5 Easy-to-Read Plays Based on Classic Stories

SCHOLASTIC
PROFESSIONAL BOOKS

New York • Toronto • London • Auckland • Sydney
Mexico City • New Delhi • Hong Kong

All of the plays in this book originally
appeared in *Scholastic Scope* magazine

Cover design by Jaime Lucero and Vincent Ceci
Cover illustrations by Mona Mark
Interior design by Sydney Wright
Interior illustrations by David Wenzel

ISBN 0-439-04415-4

Contents

Introduction

A teenager masquerading as a prince, a mad scientist creating an evil creature, and a lost world filled with dinosaurs—each of the plays in this book features characters and plots that are sure to captivate your students. The interactive and engaging play format will bring classic stories to life and provide an ideal introduction to distinguished writers Mark Twain, Nathaniel Hawthorne, Charles Dickens, Sir Arthur Conan Doyle, and Mary Shelley.

The plays cover a wide range of styles and genres—from Mark Twain's humorous "The Prince and the Pauper" to Mary Shelley's gothic horror story "Frankenstein"—and can be used in countless ways. Incorporate Dickens' "The Life and Adventures of Nicholas Nickleby" into a unit on English history or the Industrial Revolution. Add "Frankenstein" to a science fiction genre study. Introduce Early American literature with Hawthorne's "The Birthmark." Or simply enrich your language arts program by using the plays for readers' theater.

Each play is followed by a Teaching Guide, which includes a biographical sketch of the author, discussion questions for after reading, extension activities, plus a list of other books of interest.

Enjoy!

The Life and Adventures of Nicholas Nickleby

Dramatized by Adrienne Su from the
classic novel by Charles Dickens

◆ Characters ◆

Nicholas Nickleby: an 18-year-old

Kate Nickleby: his 16-year-old sister

Mrs. Nickleby: Nicholas and Kate's mother

Ralph Nickleby: uncle of Nicholas and Kate

Newman Noggs: Ralph's assistant

Wackford Squeers: schoolmaster

Smike: an orphan

Madeline Bray: a young woman

Walter Bray: Madeline's father

Arthur Gride

Peg: Gride's housekeeper

Charles & Ned Cheeryble: twin brothers

Students of Dotheboys Hall: all boys

Lord Frederick Verisopht

Sir Mulberry Hawk

Mrs. Wititterly

Vincent Crummles

Mr. Brooker

Mr. Snawley

Narrator

Scene 1

Narrator: In the 1830s Mr. Nickleby died after losing all his money. Penniless, Mrs. Nickleby and her children, Nicholas and Kate, move to London, hoping to get help from Mr. Nickleby's rich brother Ralph. But when Ralph comes to their pitiful, temporary apartment, he acts very cold.

Ralph *(to Mrs. Nickleby):* How are you?

Mrs. Nickleby *(dabbing her eyes):* Mine was no common loss, sir.

Ralph: It was no uncommon loss, ma'am. Husbands die every day, and wives, too.

Nicholas *(angrily):* And brothers, too.

Ralph: Yes, sir, and puppies, likewise. *(Looks at Nicholas)* How old is this boy?

Mrs. Nickleby: Nicholas is nearly 19.

Ralph: And what will you do for a living?

Nicholas: Anything—except live off my mother.

Ralph *(to Mrs. Nickleby):* Well, ma'am, you tell me there's nothing left for you?

Mrs. Nickleby: Nothing.

Ralph *(sighing):* I don't know how it is, but whenever a man dies without any property of his own, he always seems to think he has a right to dispose of other people's. Can your daughter earn a living?

Mrs. Nickleby: Kate has been well educated.

Kate: I'll work hard for food and shelter.

Ralph *(to Nicholas):* You're willing to work?

Nicholas: Of course I am.

Ralph: I know just the job for you, Nicholas. I will find something for Kate as well. Meanwhile you may move into an abandoned house I own—until it is rented out.

Narrator: Ralph leaves. The family feels hopeful—not knowing that Ralph, a greedy man who has gotten his money in distasteful ways, just wants to get rid of them.

Scene 2

Narrator: Ralph arranges for Nicholas to work at Dotheboys Hall, a boarding school in a remote part of England, where he will assist the schoolmaster, Mr. Squeers. Nicholas watches Mr. Squeers call to order a roomful of boys who are all dressed in rags.

Squeers: Now, where's young Jones?

Student #1: You told him to clean the windows, sir.

Squeers: Good! Where's young Smike?

Student #2: He's weeding the garden, sir.

Squeers: And you, boy, what's a horse?

Student #3: A beast, sir.

Squeers: Of course it is. That's your lesson for today. Now, class, go draw water until we tell you to stop.

Narrator: The boys wearily leave the room. Nicholas is amazed by how ill-fed and sad they look. That night, he reads a letter he has received from Newman Noggs, Uncle Ralph's worn-out assistant.

Noggs *(in the letter):* "My dear young man, your father was once very kind to me. You do not know the world, or you would not be bound to this horrible school and master. You will need to come back to London. When you do, come to my humble flat. Best regards, Newman Noggs."

Narrator: Puzzled, Nicholas puts the letter in his pocket. The next day, as he worries about Kate and his mother, he notices one of the boys, Smike, sitting by the fireplace. Smike shrinks back.

Nicholas: Don't be afraid. Are you cold?

Smike *(shivering):* N-n-o.

Nicholas: Poor fellow!

Smike *(suddenly crying):* How many of them! How many since I was a child!

Nicholas: What are you talking about?

Smike: My friends. How they have suffered here! One boy died—

Narrator: Smike runs out of the room.

Scene 3

Narrator: Meanwhile, Kate works long hours—for pennies—for a dress-maker her uncle knows. One day, her uncle invites her to dinner. When she arrives at the house, she notices something strange.

Kate: Uncle, are there any ladies here?

Ralph: No. I don't know any.

Narrator: When dinner is served, Kate finds herself far from her uncle and surrounded by leering men. Ralph introduces her.

Ralph: Lord Frederick Verisopht, my niece!

Narrator: The men stare crudely at Kate, who draws as far away from them as she can.

Verisopht: Miss . . . Miss . . . ?

Ralph: My niece, my lord.

Verisopht *(licking his lips lewdly):* I'm sure we'll be great friends.

Hawk: Introduce me, Nickleby.

Ralph: Sir Mulberry Hawk.

Narrator: At dinner, the men make rude advances to Kate, who leaves the room in tears.

Scene 4

Narrator: Back at the school, Nicholas sees more cruelty than he ever imagined. The boys work constantly and are taught as little as they are fed. One day Squeers announces that Smike has run away.

Squeers: When I find him, I'll flay him alive before all of you as an example!

Narrator: It isn't long before Smike is found and dragged back. Squeers gathers the boys again, holds Smike with one hand, and raises his whip with the other.

Squeers: Have you anything to say?

Smike: Spare me, sir!

Squeers: I'll flog you within an inch of your life—and spare you that!

Narrator: Squeers starts to whip him.

Nicholas *(roaring):* Stop!

Squeers *(astonished):* Who cried stop?

Nicholas: I did. This must not go on.

Squeers: Must not go on?

Nicholas: I will prevent it.

Narrator: Squeers hits Nicholas, who then gives him a thorough beating. The boys don't move. After this, Nicholas packs his things and leaves. With little money, he heads toward London on foot. He stops in a barn to sleep. In the morning, a figure appears before him.

Nicholas *(rubbing his eyes):* Smike?

Smike: You must let me go with you. You are my only friend. Please take me with you.

Nicholas: I am a friend who can do little for you. How did you get this far?

Smike: I followed, at a distance.

Nicholas: Poor fellow! I am nearly as poor as you. But you can go with me.

Scene 5

Narrator: After days of hard traveling, Nicholas and Smike arrive at Newman Nogg's tiny flat. Noggs welcomes them.

Noggs: You are soaked, and I—I don't even have a change of clothes to offer you.

Nicholas: I have dry clothes. I'm very sorry to bother you. But, please, how are Kate and my mother?

Noggs: Well. Both well.

Nicholas: I don't want to shock them by showing up all of a sudden, so I have imposed on you instead. I have bad news.

Narrator: Nicholas explains what happened.

Nicholas: Has my uncle heard yet?

Noggs: He's had a letter from Squeers.

Nicholas: I must go tell him the truth!

Noggs: Don't. Your uncle is out of town.

Narrator: But before long, Ralph is back in town. Nicholas tries to reach Kate and Mrs. Nickleby to tell them what happened before Ralph does. But Ralph is already there.

Ralph: This is the situation. I recommended him, against my better judgment, to a man for whom he might have worked in comfort for years. What is the result? A violent attack on the man—and the abduction of one of the boys!

Kate: I never will believe it!

Mrs. Nickleby: He must be innocent!

Ralph: Then why hasn't he shown his face? Do innocent men just disappear? Assault, riot, kidnapping: what do you call these?

Nicholas *(bursting in):* Lies!

Narrator: Everyone is shocked. Ralph is the first to recover.

Ralph: Lies? You attacked your master and nearly killed him! And kidnapped a boy!

Nicholas: I interfered to save a miserable boy from the worst cruelty I've even seen. If it happened again, I'd do the same. The boy is with me now, and I have no plans to return him to that abusive place.

Ralph: You will not receive another penny's help from me! Nor will your mother and sister if you stay here!

Nicholas: I don't want any more of your help. Mother, Kate, I must go. If I stay, I will only bring you more suffering. You will hear from me when I am better off.

Scene 6

Narrator: Nicholas and Smike walk for two days toward Portsmouth. On the way, they see two boy actors fighting a duel. One boy is much taller than the other, but the short boy wins easily. Vincent Crummles is there, cheering.

Crummles *(to Nicholas):* What did you think of that, sir?

Nicholas: Very good, indeed.

Crummles: You won't see boys as good as that very often, I think.

Nicholas: True. If they were only a little better matched—

Crummles: Matched! How are you supposed to get an audience's sympathy without putting one player at a huge disadvantage?

Nicholas: I see. I beg your pardon.

Crummles: Our play opens at Portsmouth the day after tomorrow. If you're going there, look into the theater and see what you think. You are going that way?

Nicholas: Yes. Yes, I am.

Crummles *(looking at Smike):* Your friend—he'd be perfect for the part of the starved man! Tell me, what takes you to Portsmouth?

Nicholas: We were hoping to find jobs . . .

Crummles: Why not join my theater company? For a pound a week?

Nicholas: Wonderful!

Crummles: I'll double that if we do well.

Scene 7

Narrator: As for Kate, she loses her job when the dressmaker she works for goes bankrupt. But she soon finds work as a companion to a woman named Mrs. Wititterly. Kate has not been with her long before Hawk and Verisopht begin dropping in every day.

Hawk *(to Mrs. Wititterly):* Miss Nickleby was always handsome, but, upon my soul, ma'am, you are much the beauty as well!

Mrs. Wititterly *(batting her eyes):* Oh!

Verisopht: She reminds one of a duchess.

Mrs. Wititterly: Oh, my!

Hawk: Or a countess!

Narrator: Mrs. Wititterly is speechless with delight. Smiling, the evil Hawk leans indecently close to Kate. Kate recoils in disgust. The minute her workday is over, Kate runs to see her uncle. Noggs sends her in to Ralph, who can see she is upset.

Ralph *(coolly):* What is the matter?

Kate: I have been wronged, insulted, and outraged—by your friends.

Ralph: Friends! I have no friends, girl.

Kate *(fiercely):* By those men I met here, then! You know what kind of people they are. I cannot bear their insults. You have influence with those vile creatures. Only you could have told them where to find me. Now tell them to leave me alone!

Ralph: I'm afraid I cannot.

Kate: What!

Ralph: We are connected in business. I can't afford to offend them.

Narrator: Kate stalks out of the room. Tears run down her face. Noggs, who has been listening, is also weeping.

Noggs *(whispering):* Don't cry. Don't cry.

Narrator: Meanwhile, Nicholas has become the star of the play and Victor Crummles' theater company has had full audiences for the first time. Nicholas has made enough money to support himself and Smike—and to save a little. Then he gets a letter from Noggs, urging him to come to London. When he and Smike go to Noggs' home, Noggs tells them what has happened to Kate. Outraged, Nicholas goes to Mrs. Wititterly's house. Kate opens the door.

Kate: Nicholas!

Nicholas *(embracing her):* How pale you are!

Kate: I have been so unhappy here. So very, very miserable. Don't leave me here.

Nicholas: I won't! Who should I

speak to about ending your stay here?

Narrator: Kate leads Nicholas inside. After settling accounts, Nicholas and Kate leave and move Mrs. Nickleby out of the house Ralph owns. They want nothing more to do with him and send him a letter saying so.

Scene 8

Narrator: The next day, Squeers limps into Ralph's office. Noggs listens in the back.

Ralph: Have you recovered from that terrible boy's attack?

Squeers: I'm all right. The medical bill was high, but I paid it.

Narrator: Ralph raises his eyebrows.

Squeers *(smiling):* Didn't cost me a penny. We picked out five boys who had never had scarlet fever, and we sent one to a family who'd got it—so he got it too. Then we put the four others to sleep in his room, and they all got it, and we had to call in the doctor. I just added a little to each of the five bills, and the parents paid it. *(Laughs.)*

Ralph: A good plan.

Squeers: Now, Nickleby. I just wondered if you could make me any compensation . . .

Narrator: Ralph looks suspicious.

Squeers: . . . besides the little you sent. Your nephew took a valuable boy from us.

Ralph: How old is this boy?

Squeers: Well, let's see. Nine years ago, a strange man left him at the school. The boy was five them. The man paid for him to stay for six years, but then no more money ever came. We couldn't find the man, so we kept the boy out of, uh, uh—

Ralph: Charity?

Squeers: Charity. He had just reached the age where he could be useful for work when your nephew ran off with him.

Scene 9

Narrator: Having settled his mother, Kate, and Smike into a new home, Nicholas goes to look for a job. He is reading signs at an employment agency when he meets the eye of a kind-looking old man.

Nicholas: A great many opportunities here.

Charles: A great many unlucky people have thought so, I dare say.

Nicholas: Oh! You aren't—

Charles *(kindly):* You thought I was looking for a job! *(Laughs)* A very

natural thought. I thought the same about you.

Nicholas: You would be right about me.

Charles: A well-behaved young gentleman like you, about to be cheated by these people? How can it be? *(Noticing that Nicholas is dressed in mourning clothes)* Eh? Who are you mourning?

Nicholas: My father.

Charles: Ah. Bad thing for a young man to lose his father. Widowed mother, too?

Nicholas: Yes.

Charles: Poor thing. Brothers? Sisters?

Narrator: Nicholas tells his whole story to the man, who then hurries him through the streets without explanation. The man leads Nicholas to a fine office, where he calls his identical twin brother, Ned Cheeryble.

Charles: Brother Ned, here is a young friend whom we must assist. We must make inquiries, of course, although I'm sure that everything he says is the truth.

Ned: It is enough, my dear brother, that you say it is. Where is Tim Linkinwater?

Charles: I've a plan, dear brother. Tim has been a faithful employee of ours for 44 years and, as a favor, we could lighten his duties and hire this gentleman to help him.

Ned: Certainly, certainly.

Charles: And I think we should rent that little cottage at Bow to him and his family. At a reduced rent, of course.

Ned: At no rent at all!

Narrator: All afternoon, the Cheeryble brothers pile kindnesses upon Nicholas. Nicholas begins bookkeeping for the two, whose business is to assist people who have not made the fortunes that they have. Later, going into Charles's office, Nicholas sees a beautiful, anxious-looking girl kneeling before Charles's desk.

Charles: My dear young lady, please rise.

Nicholas: Oh! I'm sorry!

Narrator: Nicholas excuses himself and rushes out of the room, but not before he falls madly in love with the girl. For weeks, he tries to learn something about her, but no one will tell him.

Scene 10

Narrator: One evening, Ralph is walking alone down the street. It starts raining, so he seeks shelter under a tree. A tattered man steps into his path.

Brooker (*hoarsely*): Mr. Nickleby.

Narrator: Ralph says nothing.

Brooker: I don't look much like I did eight years ago, do I?

Ralph (*recognizing him*): Not that different.

Brooker: You haven't changed a bit.

Ralph: Did you expect me to?

Brooker: Will you listen to me a minute?

Ralph: I have to wait for the rain to let up anyway, so I might as well.

Brooker: We were once in business together. When I asked for my share of the profits, you dug up an old debt of mine. You charged me 50 percent interest.

Ralph: So what of it?

Brooker: So, with the choice of going to jail or paying it, I paid it, and was ruined. You see me now with nothing to eat—and rags for clothes.

Ralph: You had your wages. And you still owe me money.

Brooker: I did not forget your betrayal. I have some information that you would give all you own to know. What will you pay me for this information? I do not ask a lot. I only need food and drink.

Ralph: Hard work never taught you anything.

Brooker: Are those of your name dear to you?

Narrator: Ralph thinks Brooker is referring to Nicholas and his family, but he is not.

Ralph: They are not. Good-bye, Brooker.

Narrator: Ralph walks away in the rain.

Scene 11

Narrator: The next day, Nicholas, Kate, Mrs. Nickleby, and Smike are having dinner when Ralph knocks on their door.

Ralph: I come on a noble mission: to restore a child to his parent.

Narrator: Ralph reaches toward Smike.

Nicholas: Out of my house! You're lying!

Narrator: At that moment, Squeers walks in, and so does a strange man, Mr. Snawley.

Squeers: We have his father here!

Narrator: Snawley runs toward Smike and clamps an arm around the boy's neck.

Snawley: Here he is, my son, my flesh and blood! How I've wanted to punish him for running away from his best friends, his teachers and masters!

Squeers: That's parental instinct, sir.

Snawley: Indeed, it's the natural feeling of beasts and birds, except for rabbits and cats, which sometimes eat their offspring.

Nicholas: If he is your son, tell me if you honestly intend to send him back to that loathsome den from which I rescued him!

Ralph *(ignoring the remark)*: There's proof of his parentage. Here are the documents.

Kate *(to Nicholas)*: Can this be true?

Nicholas *(examining a paper)*: I fear it is.

Squeers *(to Smike)*: Are you ready to go?

Smike *(clinging to Nicholas)*: No, no, no.

Snawley: I want my son.

Nicholas: Your son chooses to remain here.

Snawley *(to Smike)*: Won't you come home?

Smike: No, no, no.

Narrator: Ralph fumes and sputters. He, Squeers, and Snawley leave.

Scene 12

Narrator: Later, in the Cheeryble office, Charles talks with Nicholas.

Charles: You may remember a young woman who visited the office some weeks ago. You saw her briefly and hurried away.

Nicholas *(hopefully):* Yes, I remember her.

Charles: Her name is Madeline Bray. Her late mother was a friend of ours. Her father, who squandered the family's money, now lives in hiding from his creditors.

Nicholas: Oh, no.

Charles: The daughter lives in poverty with her father, who is ill. She tries to support him and herself by sewing, but it's not enough. Her father won't accept help.

Nicholas: Is he kind to her?

Charles: Kindness is not in his nature. Mr. Nickleby, you are the only one of our staff he does not know. We want you to go to the house and order some of her needlecraft. We will pretend to have sold it at a profit and give those profits to her.

Nicholas: Of course. Of course.

Narrator: Nicholas goes to the Bray house. Madeline meets him at the door. Mr. Bray sits in the back of the room.

Mr. Bray *(gruffly):* Who is it, Madeline?

Nicholas: I have come about some painted velvet. Here is the payment, in advance.

Narrator: He gives Madeline an envelope.

Bray: See that the money is right, Madeline.

Madeline: It's quite right, Papa, I'm sure.

Bray: Let me see.

Narrator: Madeline gives him the envelope. Bray counts the money.

Nicholas: When shall I call again?

Bray: When you're asked and not before.

Scene 13

Narrator: Noggs is working in the back room of Ralph's office. He hears Ralph and another man, Arthur Gride, come in.

Ralph: Noggs! Where is that fellow Noggs?

Narrator: Noggs doesn't answer.

Ralph: Gone to his dinner, I guess.

Gride: What would you say to me, if I was to tell you that I was going to be married?

Ralph: It must to an old hag.

Gride: No, no. To a young, beautiful girl, with dark eyes and a gorgeous face!

Ralph: At your age? Why would a young girl marry you? And why have you come to me?

Gride: Well, her name is Madeline Bray.

Ralph: So?

Gride: You know her father, Walter Bray.

Ralph: Walter Bray! He owes me money!

Gride: And me, too. Now, I haven't exactly spoken with him. I'm thinking, if I could offer him a way out of debt, plus some sort of living allowance, he might give his consent. And if he wants the money badly enough, his daughter will have no choice.

Ralph: Why should I care?

Gride: Well, I happen to know something about her that she doesn't know. She is entitled to an inheritance that will become hers when she is married.

Ralph: Hmmm.

Gride: Now, if I can get my hands on that inheritance, I'll pay back my old debt to you, with double the interest.

Ralph (*thoughtfully*): Ah-ha.

Narrator: Noggs shakes his head sadly.

Noggs (*quietly*): Poor girl, whoever she is.

Narrator: Two days later, Noggs and Nicholas walk down the street. Nicholas is preoccupied. One reason is that Smike is very ill—but that isn't the only reason.

Nicholas: I am madly in love with a girl who does not even know my name.

Noggs: I take it you know hers, though.

Nicholas: Yes. It is Madeline Bray.

Narrator: Noggs sputters and nearly chokes.

Nicholas: What's wrong?

Noggs: How can you just stand there and not even try to save her?

Nicholas: What are you talking about?

Noggs: Don't you know that within one day, she is to be married to an evil man?

Narrator: As soon as Noggs explains,

Nicholas charges down the road to the Bray house and places another order. When he is done, Madeline walks him to the door.

Nicholas *(whispering):* Miss Bray, I beg you not to go through with that marriage. The man is evil. He will ruin you.

Madeline: Sir, I have no choice.

Nicholas: You do! Delay the wedding!

Madeline: I can't. The sooner I marry, the sooner my father will have a better place to live. He can't stay here, or he'll die.

Scene 14

Narrator: The next day, Ralph and Gride go to the Bray house. Mr. Bray tells them to wait while he gets his daughter, who is sick. Bray staggers up the stairs.

Ralph: Well, Gride, you won't be paying to support that fellow for long.

Narrator: Gride laughs. The door opens, and both men look up, expecting to see Madeline. Instead, they see Nicholas and Kate.

Ralph *(sputtering):* Liar! Scoundrel! What are you doing here? *(to Kate)* Go on out, while we punish this boy as he deserves!

Kate: I'm not going anywhere.

Ralph: What are you doing here?

Nicholas: We've come to offer a home to the victim of your schemes. Let her decide.

Ralph: Scoundrel! Gride, call down Bray!

Nicholas: If you value your life, don't move!

Narrator: Gride hesitates. Ralph rushes toward the door. Nicholas grabs him by the collar. A heavy thud is heard upstairs.

Madeline *(from upstairs):* My father is dead!

Scene 15

Narrator: Several changes take place after Bray's death. Madeline falls ill, and Kate tends her in the Nickleby house. Smike gets worse, and the doctor says he must be moved to the country.

Meanwhile, Ralph and Gride, defeated, return to Gride's house. They ring the bell, but the housekeeper, Peg, doesn't answer. At last Gride breaks into his own house.

Ralph: The hag must be out.

Narrator: Gride doesn't answer but

crawls around in front of a large open chest.

Gride *(jumping up):* Robbed! Robbed!

Ralph: What? Robbed of what?

Gride: That old witch—she's gone and run off with my papers!

Ralph: What papers?

Gride: Phony deeds! The will I stole that gives Madeline everything when she marries! But Peg can't read—she'd have to show all the papers to someone else. And if anyone finds out that I stole them, I'm ruined. I'll go to jail!

Narrator: Gride runs around in circles. Meanwhile, Ralph goes to his office and talks with Squeers. Figuring that Nicholas might marry Madeline, Ralph is determined to destroy the will.

Ralph: You and I both want revenge on my dastardly nephew, I dare say.

Squeers: That's the truth.

Ralph: Now, if a man could bring me one particular document and watch me set it on fire, revenge would be ours. I would pay the man 50—no, 100—pounds!

Squeers: Oh?

Narrator: The next day, Squeers assumes a false name and rents a room in the house where Peg lives. By the end of a week, he has convinced Peg that he is a lawyer who knows all about her and her old employer.

Peg: So, did the old man ever get married?

Squeers: No, he didn't.

Peg *(laughing):* Ha! And a young man came and carried off the bride, eh?

Squeers: From under his very nose.

Narrator: Peg has a hearty laugh.

Peg: He tricked and cheated me all the years I worked for him. I've got my revenge now. I took all his secret papers.

Squeers: Show me those papers, so I can tell you what to destroy. Some of those documents might get you into trouble.

Narrator: Peg takes out Gride's documents. Squeers examines them. Coming upon the Bray will, he slips it into his coat when Peg isn't looking. All of a sudden, he is hit over the head and he falls over. Newman Noggs and Frank Cheeryble, the nephew of the twin brothers, are behind him. Noggs has dealt the blow.

Scene 16

Narrator: Nicholas and Smike are relaxing in the country. Suddenly Smike, who has become sicker and sicker, starts shouting.

Smike: He's there! He's there!

Nicholas: Who? What?

Smike: The man who first brought me to Dotheboys Hall. I know it was the man! I saw him over there, behind the tree!

Narrator: Nicholas searches carefully but sees no sign of anyone.

Smike: He looked very ragged and poorly fed. But I know he was there.

Narrator: Smike sees the man a few more times, but Nicholas sees no one. Then Smike dies; Nicholas is by his side.

Scene 17

Narrator: Ralph fumes in his office.

Ralph: Where is Noggs? He's never late.

Narrator: There is a knock at the door. Charles Cheeryble comes in.

Ralph: What do you want? Be brief, sir.

Charles: Mr. Nickleby, clearly you do not know why I am here, or you would act very differently.

Ralph: Go on.

Charles: I am here on an errand of mercy.

Ralph: Mercy! What are you doing in my house, saying you are treating me with mercy?

Charles: Come to my office, then, if you would like to hear the full story. But come quickly, or it may be too late for you.

Narrator: Charles walks out. Ralph begins to worry. He tries to locate Snawley, Squeers, and Gride, but none of them is home. Finally, he goes to the Cheerybles' and finds the twins and Noggs there.

Ralph *(to Noggs):* You here? Traitor!

Noggs: I a traitor? The way you treat your own family, an innocent girl, and any boy unlucky enough to be sent to your cruel schoolmaster friend, I see no reason to be your faithful employee!

Ralph *(to the group):* What do you all want?

Charles: Mr. Nickleby, last night Mr. Snawley made a confession.

Ralph: What does this have to do with me?

Ned: We know that you and Gride were using Squeers to recover some stolen documents from Gride's old housekeeper, Peg. Squeers is in jail. He was caught in possession of a stolen will relating to Madeline Bray. And

Snawley has admitted that you paid him to claim that Smike was his child. You can be jailed for fraud.

Ralph: But—

Charles: We want to give you a chance to escape. We would not like to see a Nickleby put behind bars. Leave London now. Go to the country, where you won't be found.

Ralph: Ha! Do you think I am so easily crushed? Just try to destroy me!

Narrator: Ralph walks out of the office, but he does not leave London. Later the same day, the Cheerybles summon him again.

Ned: We have some sad news for you.

Ralph: You don't mean that my nephew is dead, do you? That would be nice.

Ned: Shame on you, for talking like that! What if we were to tell you that one boy who never knew kindness in all his childhood, a boy who suffered at the hands of your greedy schoolmaster friend, had gone to his grave?

Ralph: So the boy Smike is dead? That's what you dragged me out here to hear?

Charles: Mr. Nickleby, that is not all.

Narrator: Brooker, the tattered man who had spoken to Ralph in the rain, steps out of a corner.

Ralph: What is he doing here?

Brooker: That poor boy Smike . . .

Ralph: Yes?

Brooker: . . . was your only son!

Narrator: Ralph falls into a chair.

Scene 18

Narrator: As Ralph recovers, Brooker talks. Nicholas has arrived at the office.

Brooker: About 25 years ago, there was a man who lived with his sister. Both were orphans. She kept house while he squandered the money. She was to get a large inheritance when she married. But the will said that if she married without her brother's consent, the money would go to some other relative.

The brother would not agree to let her marry anyone. Meanwhile, you, Ralph Nickleby, married the sister. But you insisted that the marriage be secret. You hoped the brother would die before the money was all spent.

Narrator: Ralph looks distressed.

Brooker *(to Ralph):* You were so anxious to keep the marriage secret—for the sake of money—that when your son was born, you sent the boy away. Your wife saw her child twice in her life. Then the two of you began to quarrel, and finally, your wife left you.

Ralph: What is the point of all this?

Brooker: I had worked with you, and you had cheated me. But for some reason, you asked me to find the child and bring him to you. I do not know why you wanted the child. Perhaps you wanted to use him to get back at your ex-wife. I found the boy, who was weak from neglect. The doctors said he should be moved to the country.

You were away, so I thought of a plan for revenge. I took the boy to a school run by a Mr. Squeers. Then I told you that your son was dead. I knew that later I could use my knowledge of the son to get revenge. It was harsh of me.

I paid the school fees for six years, but after that I could no longer pay. Three years later—only a few weeks ago—I found out that the boy had run away from the school. I went to talk to you, hoping for money in exchange for the information, but you sent me away.

Then I heard that the boy was very ill. I traveled to the country where he was said to be, and saw him resting outside. I knew the sad face instantly!

Nicholas: You must have been the man he saw! He kept saying he saw you.

Brooker: I didn't know what to do. Before I could decide, the child was dead. I am sorry. I am guilty.

Narrator: The lamp next to Ralph clatters to the floor, and the room goes dark. When the lights are put back on, Ralph is gone.

Epilogue

Narrator: In the end, Ralph Nickleby committed suicide in his office. The other Nicklebys had happier fates. Nicholas married Madeline Bray, and Kate married Frank Cheeryble. Both couples had many children. Mrs. Nickleby lived sometimes with Kate and sometimes with Nicholas. Newman Noggs lived nearby and was a great friend to the children. Nicholas was able to close down Dotheboys Hall and help all the boys find homes.

The Life and Adventures of

Nicholas Nickleby

 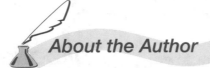 *About the Author*

Charles Dickens is one of the most popular and acclaimed English authors. His stories and characters, which include Scrooge, Oliver Twist, and David Copperfield, are as compelling today as they were to readers in the 1830s.

Charles Dickens was born in Portsmouth, England, in 1812. When Dickens was twelve, his father was thrown in debtor's prison and Dickens was forced to help support his family by working in a factory. While Dickens only worked for a short time and was able to return to school, he never forgot the experience. His novel *David Copperfield*, which tells the story of a boy who endures hard times as he grows up, was based on events and experiences from Dickens' life.

Dickens was inspired by real people, places, and situations, and his work often highlighted the social problems facing England in the 1800s, particularly the plight of impoverished and neglected children. In *The Life and Adventures of Nicholas Nickleby*, Squeers and Dotheboys Hall were based on a real headmaster and a real boarding school. Dickens had heard for many years about the horrendous conditions in boarding schools in Yorkshire, England. He went to investigate the schools firsthand and learned from a Yorkshire native about the inhumane treatment the students received. The novel *Nicholas Nickleby* helped bring the conditions in the Yorkshire boarding schools to the public's attention.

Dickens died in 1870, before he finished writing *The Mystery of Edwin Drood*. In addition to *The Life and Adventures of Nicholas Nickleby*, Dickens also wrote *The Pickwick Papers*, *The Old Curiosity Shop*, *Martin Chuzzlewit*, *Hard Times*, *Bleak House*, *A Tale of Two Cities*, *Great Expectations*, *David Copperfield*, *A Christmas Carol*, plus many other stories and novels.

 Responding to the Play

❖ In Scene 1 of the play, Ralph Nickleby states: "I don't know how it is but whenever a man dies without any property of his own, he always seems to think he has a right to dispose of other people's." What does Ralph mean by this? What does this say about his character? How much help does Ralph Nickleby really provide for Nicholas and his family?

❖ At the end of Scene 5, Nicholas leaves his mother and Kate and sets out on his own. Why does he do that? Should he have stayed with his family? What other options did he have?

❖ In Scene 10, Brooker tries to tell Ralph Nickleby something. Why doesn't Ralph listen? What was Brooker trying to tell Ralph? What might have happened if Ralph had listened to what Brooker had to say?

❖ During the course of the play, many people come to the aid of Nicholas and his family. Which characters helped Nicholas? How did they help him?

❖ Nicholas Nickleby is only eighteen years old. How is his life different from an eighteen-year-old's life today? Are there any similarities? What about Smike? What would his situation be like if he lived today? Would it be better or worse?

❖ Dickens first published many of his novels in serial format in magazines. Each issue of the magazine would feature a new chapter in the story. Do continuing stories exist today, in books, magazines, or on television? Are there any book or movie characters that you would like to read more about or follow their story from week to week?

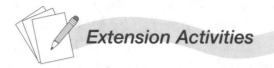

Extension Activities

Dastardly Villains and Philanthropic Friends

Ralph Nickleby, Squeers, and Gride are clearly evil characters, while Noggs and the Cheeryble brothers are good friends to Nicholas. Challenge students to compare and contrast an evil character and a kindly character by writing a brief profile of each one. To create the profiles, students can divide a large sheet of paper in half. On one side, they can write a profile of the evil character and on the other side, a profile of the kindly character. The profiles might include the character's name, occupation, evil deed or helpful act, and a remarkable quote. Students can complete their profiles with illustrations of both characters.

Create a Character Chart

Dickens' stories are filled with characters and feature complex story lines. To help students understand the connections between the characters, encourage them to create a graphic organizer that outlines how the characters are related. Using the list of characters on page 7, they might start with Nicholas and his family, add the other characters, then draw lines to show the connections between various characters. Under each character's name students might add a sentence or two noting the character's place in the story. Students can work on their graphic organizers as they read the play, adding new characters as they appear, or they can work on the chart after finishing the play.

Researching Life During Dickens' Era

In *Nicholas Nickleby,* and in many of his other stories, Dickens writes about the cruel treatment and harsh conditions children were forced to endure. During the Victorian age, when Dickens was writing, it was common for poor children to work—often in terrible conditions for very little money—and the orphanages were bleak and sometimes cruel places. Have students learn more about these issues by researching how children lived in England during the 19th century. Students can work in small groups and each group might research one of the issues addressed in the play, including child labor, schools, and orphanages. Each group can then share its findings with the class. As a follow-up, you might have students research the conditions facing children in developing nations today.

Further Reading

Students who enjoyed *The Life and Adventures of Nicholas Nickleby* might enjoy reading one of Dickens' novels. There are many abridged and illustrated versions of Dickens' work available for young readers.

David Copperfield, Dickens most autobiographical novel, follows the adventures of a young man from childhood to his adult years.

Oliver Twist tells the story of a young orphan who escapes from a workhouse and falls in with criminals.

Students might also be interested in reading the original version of the holiday favorite, *A Christmas Carol*.

The Birthmark

Adapted by Adam Grant from the short
story by Nathaniel Hawthorne

◆ Characters ◆

Narrator 1

Narrator 2

Aylmer: a great scientist

Georgiana: Aylmer's wife

Aminadab: Aylmer's lab assistant

Woman 1

Woman 2

Woman 3

Woman 4

Man 1

Man 2

Man 3

Scene 1

Narrator 1: Sometime late in the last century, there lived a young scientist and philosopher. His name was Aylmer.

Narrator 2: Of course in those days, when things like electricity, which we now consider ordinary, were brand-new discoveries, the boundaries between science and magic were not always clear. Many people thought of scientists as brilliant sorcerers with strange powers, and Aylmer was among the greatest scientists of his time.

Narrator 1: It happened one day that this great scientist left his laboratory in the hands of an assistant, washed the stain of acids from his fingers, and persuaded a beautiful woman to be his wife.

Narrator 2: She was beautiful in nearly every respect. In fact, she was almost perfect. Her one flaw was a tiny birthmark on her left cheek. But more about that later.

Narrator 1: After he was married, Aylmer seemed to change. Once the great scientist had been obsessed with his work and nothing else. But now it seemed he had two equal passions; science and his newfound love.

Aylmer *(writing)*: "Dear journal, these twin fascinations demand my constant attention. At first I feared that my new-found love might interfere with my scientific work. But now I wonder what might be created from combining the two. Perhaps through science I might give my love the gift of perfection."

Narrator 2: This was perhaps not his finest idea.

Scene 2

Narrator 1: One day soon after their marriage, Aylmer sat gazing at his wife.

Narrator 2: Something had begun to bother him, and the longer he sat quietly the worse his mood grew, until finally he spoke.

Aylmer: Georgiana, has it never occurred to you that the mark upon your cheek might be removed?

Georgiana: No indeed.

Narrator 1: She was surprised by the seriousness in his voice. He had never mentioned the mark before.

Georgiana: To tell you the truth, it has been so often called a beauty mark that I was simple enough to imagine it might be one.

Aylmer: Upon another face, perhaps it might, but never on yours. You are so nearly perfect that this slightest possible defect shocks me, being the only imperfect thing about you.

Narrator 2: Now Georgiana was deeply hurt and burst into tears.

Georgiana: Shock you, my husband! Then why did you marry me? You cannot love what shocks you!

Narrator 1: The birthmark on Georgiana's cheek was a deep reddish color, and looked exactly like a tiny hand.

Narrator 2: When she blushed, the mark would blend in with the rest of her cheek and almost disappear. But when her face returned to its normal pale shade, there was the mark again.

Narrator 1: It was not always easy to predict how people might react at first glimpse of the birthmark. Some women, jealous of her beauty, looked upon Georgiana's birthmark with suspicion.

Woman 1: Have you noticed the way she can make it disappear by causing her face to flush?

Woman 2: Nonsense. It just blends in when she blushes, that's all.

Woman 3: But when she is nervous, it becomes darker. Is it magic? Or sorcery.

Woman 2: It looks darker when her skin becomes pale, that's all. Magic, really, how ridiculous.

Woman 4: It's just hideous! How can anyone call her beautiful with that thing on her face? A bloody hand, that's what it is. Who knows where it came from or what caused it?

Narrator 2: Most men, captivated by her overall beauty, looked upon the mark quite differently.

Man 1: Perhaps at her birth, a tiny fairy laid its hand upon her cheek, leaving a token of the magic womanly charms that now cause her to conquer so many hearts.

Man 2: I would give my very life for the privilege of kissing that mysterious hand.

Man 3: I just wish it weren't there. She would be so beautiful if it weren't for that birthmark.

Narrator 1: As the months wore on, Aylmer became obsessed with the birthmark. Many nights he would find himself up late, lecturing passionately on the subject to his assistant, Aminadab.

Narrator 2: Aminadab looked more like an animal than a man. He was always filthy, as if he lived in the woods. With his great strength and Aylmer's vast intelligence, it was almost as if the two together formed one perfect man.

Aylmer: It is because she is otherwise so beautiful that the birthmark bothers me so much. You probably wouldn't understand this, but I just cannot stand to look at that one little flaw that keeps her from being truly perfect. I must get rid of it.

Narrator 1: But Aminadab did understand. In fact, he understood quite a lot. In many ways it is a shame that Aylmer never listened to what he had to say.

Aminadab *(softly):* If she were my wife I would never part with that birthmark.

Scene 3

Narrator 2: One night Aylmer found himself having a terrible nightmare. In it, he was operating on Georgiana, trying to remove the hated birthmark. But he was horrified to find that the tiny hand seemed to be clutching her very heart.

Georgiana: Aylmer, Aylmer, wake up!

Aylmer *(waking, still groggy):* What is it my love?

Georgiana: You were dreaming of the birthmark. This cannot go on. We have got to remove it no matter what happens to me. I'd rather die trying to get rid of it than go on living like this. Is there nothing you can do?

Aylmer: Yes, my dear. I had planned to tell you in the morning. I have given the matter much thought, and am now convinced that I can remove the hated mark.

Georgiana: Then do not delay. Rid me of this bloody hand. While I carry this hateful mark upon my cheek, our love can never be its fullest.

Aylmer: Noble wife, do not doubt my power. I know I can cure you of this one imperfection, and when I have, I will have tamed nature and science, and our love will be unmatched on this earth.

Narrator 1: And he tenderly kissed her cheek—her right cheek—not that which bore the crimson hand.

Scene 4

Narrator 2: The next day, Aylmer told his wife of his plan. They were to move into the apartments Aylmer kept as a laboratory, during which time he could work uninterrupted, and she could rest around the clock to prepare for the ordeal of the cure.

Narrator 1: As he led her into the apartments, Aylmer looked cheerfully into her face, to reassure her.

Aylmer: My dearest wife—

Narrator 1: But before he could finish speaking, her face passed close to his. As he saw the birthmark glide by on her cheek, he could not help letting out a violent shudder as if her had seen a ghost.

Narrator 2: Georgiana fainted when she saw the look on his face.

Aylmer: Aminadab! Aminadab!

Narrator 1: The assistant appeared.

Aylmer: Aminadab, throw open the door to her room!

Aminadab: Mmm. Yes, master.

Narrator 2: Later, when Georgiana had been carried, still sleeping, into her rooms, Aylmer began his delicate work.

Aylmer: Aminadab, I will need complete solitude in order to complete the necessary calculations.

Aminadab: Mmm. Yes, master.

Aylmer: Georgiana's rooms must be fixed so that she is entirely comfortable and content. Go find the finest drapes and carpets you can, buy oil-burning lamps and fancy picture frames. We must do everything possible to transform the ugly, drafty chambers into an agreeable suite for a lady.

Aminadab: Mmm. Yes, master.

Aylmer *(writing):* "Dear journal, I must now commit myself entirely to my scientific work in order to create a cure powerful enough to kill the hateful hand that clutches the cheek of my beloved."

Scene 5

Narrator 1: When she awoke, Georgiana indeed found herself in a beautiful and mysterious chamber. She felt as if she were resting in a pavilion in the clouds. As time passed, however, a terrible combination of boredom and dread set over her.

Narrator 2: A few hours later, the scientist emerged from his secret lab to visit his lovely patient.

Aylmer: How are you feeling tonight, my dear?

Georgiana: Just fine, thank you. A little tired.

Aylmer: Do you feel especially hot or cold? Do you feel any unfamiliar tingling sensations or a shortness of breath?

Georgiana: No, my husband, I'm perfectly comfortable. Why do you ask?

Aylmer: Oh, no reason, I just want you to be comfortable. Sometimes these old buildings, uh. . . Excuse me. I must get back to work.

Narrator 1: The next few days were the same for Georgiana: Hours of boredom and loneliness followed by a brief interview with her husband and then more waiting. Georgiana began to wonder if perhaps her treatment had already begun, in the form of medications given her through her food and drink.

Narrator 2: Once, just after Aylmer had left her room, Georgiana realized that she had forgotten to tell him about a symptom she was feeling, and quietly followed him to his secret laboratory. She found him there with Aminadab. He looked tired and worried, as he huddled over a boiling beaker on his stove.

Aylmer: Careful now Aminadab. We are in the laboratory, not the forest. We must concentrate at all times.

Narrator 1: The assistant was the first to see Georgiana.

Aminadab: Look, master, look!

Aylmer: Georgiana, why do you come here? Have you no trust in me? Would you bring that terrible birthmark in here to disturb my work?

Georgiana: No, my love, it is I who should complain. You do not trust me. I now see a terrible look of fear on your face that I have never seen before. You are keeping secrets from me about the birthmark. Think better of me, husband. Tell me all the risk that we run in this. I will not faint or shrink in terror.

Aylmer: Noble wife, I never knew how strong you were until this moment. I will tell you. The crimson hand clutches your cheek, your entire being, with a power that I never expected. I have already tried to destroy it with all the known cures. Only one thing remains to be tried. If that does not work, we are ruined!

Georgiana: But why have you not yet tried that final cure?

Aylmer: Because, dear wife, there is great danger in it.

Georgiana: Danger? There is only one danger, that this hideous mark will stain my face forever and drive us both insane!

Aylmer: Heaven knows you are right. Return to your bedroom, and the medicine will be brought in soon.

Narrator 2: When Aylmer arrived in Georgiana's chamber, he carried a crystal goblet containing a liquid as colorless as water. She greeted him with a peaceful but serious look.

Aylmer: The composition of this potion is perfect. Unless all my science deceives me, this cannot fail.

Georgiana: I need no proof. Give me the goblet. I will gladly trust you with my life.

Aylmer: Drink then. And soon you will look as perfect as your soul already is.

Narrator 1: Georgiana drank it all in one sip, after which she fell immediately into a deep sleep.

Scene 6

Narrator 2: Aylmer sat quietly at the edge of his wife's bed, watching her intensely while she slept. Every movement of her closed eyes, every slight change, he recorded carefully into his journal.

Narrator 1: At first there was little to record, but soon the miracle began. Sure enough, slowly and steadily, the crimson hand began to fade.

Aylmer *(writing):* "Dear journal, twenty minutes ago, the beastly hand was deepest crimson, but now it is almost gone. Even as I write, I cannot keep up with the progress being made. Now it is so faint that the slightest blush of her cheek would make it invisible. I have done it."

Narrator 2: As he looked at his beautiful sleeping wife, a smile formed on his face, and he began to laugh quietly to himself.

Aylmer: Come, Aminadab, share this laugh with me! We have done it. We are victorious together!

Narrator 1: These exclamations broke Georgiana's sleep. A slight smile crossed her lips as she caught her reflection in the mirror and saw for the first time the absence of that dreaded mark.

Narrator 2: But soon that smile was replaced by a look of fear and sadness.

Georgiana: My poor Aylmer.

Aylmer: Poor? No, richest! Happiest! Most favored! My peerless bride, we are successful. You are perfect!

Georgiana: Not perfect, my Aylmer. Don't you see? You have tried to create perfection on earth. Perhaps it is just not possible. Please never regret striving for the heavens. You had the best of intentions. But farewell, Aylmer. I am dying.

Narrator 1: It was true. She was dying. Perhaps the hated hand really was grasping her heart. Maybe it was connected to her lungs, we will never know for sure. What we do know is that she simply could not live without it.

Narrator 2: As the last crimson tint of the birthmark passed from her cheek, so the last breath of her life passed from her lips. Her soul lingered a moment near her husband, and flew heavenward. She was gone.

Narrator 1: As Aylmer sat with his head in his hands, he could almost hear Aminadab's hoarse chuckle again, but he was too lost in thought to respond. Perhaps a little of his own life had escaped that day as well.

Narrator 2: How could a man of his intelligence have thrown away love and happiness in the shallow search for physical perfection? Could he not recognize real beauty?

The Birthmark

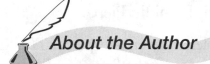
About the Author

Nathaniel Hawthorne was born in Salem, Massachusetts, in 1804. His ancestors were prominent figures in the early days of the Massachusetts Bay Colony, and one of them was a judge at the Salem witch trials. Hawthorne's father died when he was four, leaving his family little to live on.

Hawthorne attended Bowdoin College in Maine, where he became friends with the poet Henry Wadsworth Longfellow and the future president Franklin Pierce. After graduating in 1825, Hawthorne returned to Salem to begin his career as a writer. He published his first novel, *Fanshawe: A Tale* in 1828. The book was not well received and Hawthorne considered it a failure—he even tried to collect and destroy all the copies of it.

Hawthorne continued writing and eventually began publishing his stories in periodicals and anthologies. When he was 32, Hawthorne published his first collection of stories, *Twice-Told Tales.*

"The Birthmark" was published in his next book of stories, *Mosses From an Old Manse*. The Old Manse in the title refers to the house in Concord, Massachusetts, where Hawthorne and his wife Sophia spent the first years of their marriage and where Hawthorne wrote the stories in the collection.

Hawthorne was never able to completely support himself with his writing and held many jobs during his lifetime, including working at the Boston Custom House. He lived for a few years in England when he was appointed the U.S. consul by President Franklin Pierce.

In 1850, Hawthorne completed his masterpiece, *The Scarlet Letter*. His other works include *The House of the Seven Gables, The Blithedale Romance*, and *The Marble Faun*. He also wrote books for children including *A Wonder-Book for Books and Girls* (1852) and *Tanglewood Tales for Boys and Girls* (1853). Much of Hawthorne's work explores issues of morality and good and evil. "The Birthmark," which examines human imperfection, is a excellent introduction to one of America's greatest writers.

 ### Responding to the Play

❖ What does Georgiana think about her birthmark at the beginning of the play? How do her feelings change as the play continues? Can you identify three statements by Georgiana that show how her feelings change during the course of the play? What other opinions do people express about the birthmark?

❖ At the end of Scene 2, Aminadab states: "If she were my wife I would never part with that birthmark?" Why do you think Aminadab sees things differently? Why doesn't Aylmer listen to Aminadab?

❖ At one point, Aylmer states: "Noble wife, do not doubt my power. I know I can cure you of this one imperfection, and when I have, I will have tamed nature and science, and our love will be unmatched on this earth." What does Aylmer think his source of power is? Was he able to tame nature and science?

❖ In the last scene of the play, Georgiana says to Aylmer: "Please never regret striving for the heavens. You had the best of intentions." Do you agree with Georgiana, did Aylmer have the best intentions? Do you think Aylmer will regret what he did?

❖ In this story, Aylmer seeks perfection. Do people today seek perfection in the same way? How? How do you think the author would react to the way people try to change their appearances today?

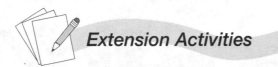 Extension Activities

Exploring Viewpoints

Have students pick either Georgiana or Aminidab and write a version of the story from his or her point of view. Students can construct their stories as journal entries, creating two or three entries that describe major events or turning points in the play.

Modern Tales

Challenge students to create a modern-day version of "The Birthmark." Divide the class into small groups and explain that each group will be responsible for transforming "The Birthmark" into a story that takes place today. Tell students that playwrights and filmmakers often put a new spin on classic stories by changing the setting and time period. For example, *West Side Story* is a version of *Romeo and Juliet,* and the movie *Roxanne* is an updated version of *Cyrano de Bergerac.* As they adapt the play, students should stick to the basic plot outline but can make any other changes they see fit, including changing the characters' names, personalities, or professions. Each group can present its version of the play to the class. After, discuss as a class how each group has chosen to update the story.

What's the Moral of the Story?

In "The Birthmark" Hawthorne seems to be trying to convey a message or a moral to his readers. Ask students to each write one sentence that summarizes what they think the moral or lesson is in "The Birthmark." Students should try to make the sentence—like the moral of a fable—concise and easy-to-understand. Ask students to share their sentences and discuss them as a class.

A Meeting of the Scientists: Frankenstein & Aylmer

If students have also read *Frankenstein*, ask them imagine a conversation between the characters Frankenstein and Alymer. Students can set the conversation either before or after the stories take place. Possibilities might include: Aylmer meets Frankenstein after Georgiana has died but before Frankenstein had created his monster, or the characters meet as young university students. Students might want to work with partners to create the dialogue and then act out the meeting in front of the class.

Further Reading

Hawthorne's two collections of short stories, *Twice-Told Tales* and *Mosses from an Old Manse*, feature more short stories students will enjoy. For a different twist on the mad scientist tale, students should read Hawthorne's "Rappaccini's Daughter." Other popular Hawthorne stories include "Young Goodman Brown," "The Minister's Black Veil," and "My Kinsman, Major Molineux."

Frankenstein

Adapted by Gary Drevitch from the
classic novel by Mary Shelley

◆ Characters ◆

Captain Robert Walton

Victor Frankenstein: A scientist

Narrator: Victor telling his story

Elizabeth Lavenza: Victor's fiancée

Henry Clerval: Victor's best friend

The Creature

Alphonse Frankenstein: Victor's father

Mr. DeLacey

Mr. Kirwin

Scene 1

Walton *(writing):* "Captain's log, August 20, 1798: As we sailed through the Arctic Ocean in search of the North Pole, we rescued a man trapped on the ice in a beat-up dogsled. On board, I asked the man—who was near death—why he was traveling alone in the Arctic."

Victor: I am trying to capture someone who fled from me.

Walton: Yesterday we saw a dogteam pulling a single man on a sled across the ice.

Victor: That must be the creature. Swear to me that if this ship meets him—and if I am already dead—you will kill him. It's for the good of humanity!

Walton: My friend, this ship has just one mission. We must find the North Pole; we have no time for anything else. I'd give my life to discover the knowledge that I know lies ahead.

Victor: Are you as crazed for knowledge as I once was? Hear my tale, and then end your search for knowledge!

Scene 2

Narrator: When I turned 17, I left my family in Geneva to study in Germany.

But I hated to leave my fiancée, Elizabeth.

Elizabeth: Victor, I'll miss you so much. But I know that your happiness depends upon your scientific work, and I want you to be happy.

Narrator: I knew Elizabeth—who had been adopted as a child by my late mother—was right. So I went off to school and studied night and day. It may seem unbelievable, but after months of research in biology, chemistry, and electricity, I discovered how to give life to lifeless human matter! I could create a person from the organs of the dead! My best friend, Henry, was at school with me, and I told him about my discoveries.

Henry: How can this be? It's impossible!

Victor: It's difficult but not impossible. One problem is the small size of most human parts. My creation—when I make him—must be at least eight feet tall.

Henry *(shuddering):* But how will you get your "materials?"

Victor: I'll do whatever I have to—even rob fresh graves and hospital morgues. I must if I want to reach my goals. I want to pour light into our dark world! I will create a new, happy species of man.

Henry: Victor, I must tell you: Your ideas are not only impossible, they're wrong! Morally wrong!

Narrator: But I did not listen to my friend's words. Instead, I went on with my experiments. The first ones were failures. It tore at my soul to throw away the parts that I'd used in my work, but for two sleepless years, I never stopped. Finally, on a dreary November night, I succeeded. But before I could even stop to examine my creation, I heard my name called. Henry had stumbled into my laboratory and he saw my creation.

Henry *(in horror):* What have you done? You did not listen to me. You've created a monster!

Narrator: It was true. I wanted to make him beautiful, but he was far from human. His yellowed skin barely stretched over his facial muscles. His eyes were as white as their sockets. His lips were black. The creature grinned and opened his jaws to utter some sounds, but I did not stay to hear his words. I was disgusted by him—and frightened.

Victor: Henry, run! I can't look at it!

Narrator: We ran from my laboratory into the wet night. The next morning, our courage returned and we went back. It was my secret hope that the creature would be gone. I hoped it had fallen to its death in the river. I slowly approached my door and then threw it open. The room was empty! I clapped my hands in joy.

Victor: Henry, we must never speak of this to anyone.

Henry: I pray that you have learned your lesson. Never try such an experiment again!

Scene 3

Narrator: In the months that followed, I conducted no more experiments. Then my father sent me a tragic letter.

Alphonse *(in the letter):* "Victor, I wanted to keep this news from you until you came back next month. But that would have been a cruel kindness. The truth is that your little brother William has been murdered—strangled! Elizabeth blames herself. Please come home and comfort her."

Narrator: It had been six years since I left home. I rushed back to learn more of my youngest brother's murder.

Elizabeth: It's all my fault! The night William was murdered, I allowed him to wear a locket of your mother's as he walked in the fields. The killer must have murdered him in order to steal it. William's death is my fault. Victor, how can I go on?

Alphonse: Victor, the authorities have discovered the murderer—

Elizabeth: It's not true! They arrested William's poor nanny, Justine Moritz. She has been with us for four years. She wouldn't have killed William. She loved him!

Alphonse: Your mother's locket was found in Justine's coat. She claims to have no idea how it got there, but lately she has been terribly ill with fever. She walks in her sleep, and cannot account for her actions.

Elizabeth: Victor, they'll try her in court tomorrow! Can't you help her? They'll sentence her to death!

Victor: I know you're right. No one who knew William could have killed him. The killer must have planted the locket on Justine as she walked in her sleep.

Narrator: That night I walked through a thunderstorm in the hills, wondering what fiend could have killed my brother. Suddenly, a flash of lightning revealed the face of the killer standing across the hills. It was a face I hadn't seen for two years—the face of the creature I created! So I myself was the cause of William's death! I tried to chase the creature, but he ran off at amazing speed. For the first time, I understood the evil I had turned loose

on the world. I ran inside.

Victor: Father! Elizabeth! Justine is innocent! I know who killed William! I have just seen him!

Alphonse: Son, who is it?

Narrator: I froze. How could I tell them the killer's identity without also telling them a story they could never believe? I said I was ill and went to bed. The next day, Justine was hung—the second victim of my horrible experiment. I left home again to seek peace in the Austrian hills.

Scene 4

Narrator: On a chilly day two weeks later, an enormous man sped toward me across the rocky hills. It was that villain I had created.

Victor: Leave me alone, devil! Or stay, so I can end your evil life! I only wish your death could restore your two victims!

Creature: I feared you would treat me this way. All men hate the wretched. But, creator, how can you reject me? We are bound by ties that can be broken only by death. Would you kill me after creating me?

Victor: I never should have created you! I'll kill you right here and now!

Narrator: I attacked the creature, but he easily knocked me to the ground. I knew then that I could never defeat him in combat.

Creature: In my life, I've known nothing but suffering. Still, I will defend my life. You made me taller, faster, stronger than other men. If you do what I ask of you, I'll leave you and humanity alone. If not, I'll fill an ocean with the blood of your friends. You owe me happiness.

Victor: I owe you nothing, murderer!

Creature: All men hate me on sight. Am I wrong also to hate them? I was created with a good heart. Why do I now do evil? I was rejected by my creator! And only my creator—only you—has the power to save humanity from what you have created. Won't you at least hear my story?

Victor: Speak.

Scene 5

Narrator: The creature was—is—terribly evil. Yet the sadness of his story did touch me. After he left my home the night I created him, he ran out into the cold hills. He tried to communicate with people, but only frightened them with his grunting and his horrifying appearance.

Creature: I finally stopped running and entered a cabin behind a small house where an old blind man lived with his son and daughter. I could watch and hear everything they did without being noticed. From their conversations, I learned to speak. From watching the son read to his father, I learned to read. From listening to what he read, I learned geography, religion, and history.

Victor: But how did you feed yourself?

Creature: For a year, I ate only food that I stole late in the evening. During that time, I came to love the DeLacey family. Finally I decided to meet them.

Victor: But surely your appearance would terrify them.

Creature: I waited until only the father, who could not see my face, was at home. If I could win his friendship, perhaps the rest of the family would welcome me as well.

Narrator: And so the creature knocked on DeLacey's door.

DeLacey: Who is there? Come in.

Creature: I am a traveler in search of rest. Could I sit next to your fire?

DeLacey: Make yourself at home, my friend.

Creature: I thank you for your kindness. I am a despised man. But now I hope that I will be welcomed when I meet the old friends I am waiting for.

DeLacey: Who are these friends?

Creature: You and your family! Please, save and protect me! I beg you!

DeLacey: Who are you?

Narrator: At that moment, the son and daughter returned home. The daughter took one look at the creature and fainted; the son attacked him with a stick. The creature could have killed him easily, but instead he fled in sadness and in pain. Had I done this creature an injustice by creating him?

Scene 6

Creature: I left DeLacey's village. From reading the papers in the coat I stole from your home the day I was created, I knew you lived in Geneva. I traveled there to find you. Only you could help me, even though you had already rejected me, and I hated you for it.

Victor: How could you imagine that I would befriend you? You killed my brother!

Creature: When I first saw him, I did not know who he was. But I thought that if he, a young boy with no prejudices, could learn to be my friend, then there could be hope for me. I approached him, but he screamed and

called me "monster." He said his father, Mr. Frankenstein, would kill me. Then I knew who he was. I killed him to begin my revenge upon you.

Victor: But why did Justine have his locket?

Creature: I left the locket with a young girl sleeping in a nearby field. She was lovely, but she would never offer me her love. She deserved to pay for the crime.

Creator, no human will associate with me. But, a true companion—a female of the same species as myself and as deformed—could love me. You must create this being. I will not leave you alone until you agree. For if I cannot inspire love, I will cause fear. And I have the power to destroy everyone you know.

Victor: I refuse! How can I create another being like you? The evil that the two of you could do could destroy the whole world.

Creature: I do evil only because there is no love in my life! With a companion, I'd be at peace.

Narrator: There was some sense in his argument. Perhaps my first reaction to him was the cause of the evil he had done.

Victor: I'll agree to your request, if you swear that you will never again bother any other human beings.

Creature: My companion and I will leave the world of men forever. Please begin your work. I will appear before it is finished.

Scene 7

Narrator: I knew the creature would be watching me closely, so I chose to work far from home, in Scotland. I hoped this would protect my loved ones from the creature's threats. I promised Elizabeth that we would be wed as soon as I returned. Henry traveled with me as far as London—but did not approve of my plans.

Henry: You cannot mean to create yet another monster?

Victor: I do have doubts. My earlier experiments were driven by my passion for discovery. But now, I hate to look at my tools, the body parts, even my own hands.

Henry: Please don't do as the creature asked. Even if the monster promised to leave humanity alone, the companion hasn't made any promises. And what if they had children and started a race of powerful, murderous creatures?

Victor: Do I have any choice, Henry? I don't know what to do.

Narrator: So I went to work in Scotland. Then one day I saw the creature's face at my window. He'd found

me just as he had promised. Seeing him made me realize I must destroy my newest creation before it stirred to life. I tore it apart, smashed my machinery, and hurled the parts at the creature at my window. Seeing this, he burst into the room.

Creature: How dare you destroy my hopes!

Victor: I could never create another being as evil as you.

Creature: You will do as I say! You are my creator, but you gave me the power to be your master: I order you to continue!

Victor: I won't listen to threats. Kill me if you must. My work is ended.

Creature: I won't kill you now. My revenge will be worse than that. I will be with you on your wedding night!

Narrator: And so he was gone. I left Scotland at once. I hired a boat and set sail for London. A fierce storm raged that night, and I was weary from lack of sleep and ill with fever. I passed out. When I woke, I found that my boat had reached land—though I did not know where. Some townspeople stood before me.

Victor: Good people, can you tell me the name of this town?

Kirwin: You'll find out soon, but I don't think you'll find that you like this place, murderer. You're under arrest.

Scene 8

Narrator: The man who arrested me was the town's chief of police. He said the body of a 25-year-old man had been found on the beach, strangled, the day before I arrived. He believed I was the killer.

Victor: Sir, I can prove I was nowhere near your town the day of the murder. The man who rented me my boat can tell you so.

Kirwin: You may be right. Still, I would like to see the effect that the sight of the corpse has on you. Please follow me.

Narrator: He took me to the open coffin, and there I saw my friend Henry. It was clear that he had been strangled by someone with enormous hands—the creature.

Victor: My dearest friend, has my evil also caused your death? Already, I have destroyed William and Justine, but you—

Narrator: I fell into madness. Kirwin kept me in prison, although he knew I was innocent. When I gained my senses back, two months had passed.

Kirwin: My friend, welcome back. We feared you would die from your fever. If you feel up to it, a friend has come to see you.

Narrator: I feared the creature had found me yet again!

Victor: No! Take him away! I cannot ever look upon that creature again!

Kirwin: I don't know what you're talking about. I'd think you would welcome a visit from your father, who has traveled all the way from Geneva to take you home.

Scene 9

Narrator: Halfway home to Geneva, my father handed me a note from Elizabeth.

Elizabeth *(in the note):* "My dearest, I am thankful that you have returned to health. But when you last left us, you were so unhappy. Our marriage has been my dream since the day I joined your family. But, over the years, we have been so much like brother and sister. I wonder if you can ever love me as a wife. I only want to see you happy. If that happiness will come in our marriage, I shall be joyful. If not, please tell me your honest feelings."

Narrator: I never loved Elizabeth more than at that moment. After all my time away, she still loved me. I arranged for us to be wed a week after my return, The wedding was marvelous, and we left for a honeymoon at our family's summer home. I tried to relax, but I couldn't forget the creature's threats.

Creature: I will be with you on your wedding night!

Narrator: The night we arrived, I left Elizabeth and looked outside the house to make sure that the creature was not there. Suddenly, I heard a scream. Instantly, I realized my stupidity: The creature never meant to kill me on my wedding night. It was Elizabeth! I ran inside. Grinning, he stood with her corpse at the window. Before I could move, he dropped her and ran into the hills. I returned home, crushed. The shock of Elizabeth's death killed my father. The creature now had five victims.

Scene 10

Victor *(to Walton on the ship):* And so I picked up the creature's trail and began the journey that led me to your ship. Over the years, the creature kept taunting me with clues so I wouldn't quit the chase. But I had no real hope of catching him, nor of killing him if I did. Many of the creature's clues took the form of messages scratched in trees.

Creature *(in a message):* "Follow me, slave! I run for the ices of the north, where you will suffer the icy grip of cold and frost. Do not delay, my enemy; we have yet to wrestle for our lives, and you must suffer more pain before that day arrives."

Victor *(to Walton on the ship):* I know that I am living out my final days on your ship.

Walton: I am keeping notes on your story. Could you describe the details of the experiments in which you created life?

Victor: Are you mad? Would you encourage other men to create enemies of humanity? No, Walton, no one shall ever repeat my work. In a fit of madness, I tried to create a human being. It was my duty to see after his happiness. I did not. It was my duty to protect humanity from his evil. I did not. I am a hideous failure.

Walton *(in his log):* "Soon after saying these words, Frankenstein was dead. I thought his story had ended at that moment. But that night, as I entered his cabin to prepare his corpse for burial, I found a giant, horrific creature standing over his body."

Creature: Here lies the victim of my crimes. Does it matter that I came here to ask his forgiveness? I destroyed everything he loved. Yet he suffered not one ten-thousandth as much as I did. How I hated myself after killing his friend! Then, in jealousy over his happiness, I killed his young wife. I still see her face. Never did I hate my creator as much as I now hate myself. I have no more feelings. All that remains for me is death.

Walton *(in the log):* "He sprang from the cabin window as he said this, onto a raft of ice which lay close to the ship. He was soon carried away by the waves and lost in darkness and distance."

Frankenstein

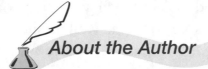

About the Author

Mary Shelley was born in London, England, in 1797. Her father, William Goodwin, was a famous philosopher and her mother, Mary Wollstonecraft, was one of the first feminists and the author of the book *A Vindication on the Rights of Women*. In 1817 Mary married the poet Percy Bysshe Shelley.

Mary Shelley was only twenty years old when she wrote Frankenstein, her first and most popular novel. *Frankenstein* began as a ghost story. During the summer of 1816, Mary, Percy Shelley, the poet Lord Byron, and other guests, were vacationing in Switzerland. One rainy weekend, Lord Byron challenged everyone to write a ghost story to share with the group.

While most of the guests never finished their stories, Mary Shelley continued to work on her ghost story. Finally, the idea came to her in a dream. Mary Shelley, describing her moment of inspiration, states: "I saw the pale student of unhallowed arts kneeling beside the thing he had put together. I saw the hideous phantasm of a man stretched out, then on the working of some powerful engine, show signs of life. His success would terrify the artist, who would rush away. . . hope that . . . this thing . . . would subside into dead matter . . . he opens his eyes; behold the horrid thing stands at his bedside, opening his curtains . . ."

Frankenstein was published in 1818. It is notable both as a gothic horror story and also as one of the first examples of science fiction. After her husband Percy Shelley drowned in 1822, Mary Shelley continued writing to support herself, publishing six novels, as well as short stories and essays. Her work includes *Valperga, The Last Man,* and *Mary Shelley: Collected Tales and Stories.*

Responding to the Play

❖ At the beginning of the play, Victor says; "Are you as crazed for knowledge as I once was? Hear my tale and then end your search for knowledge." What did Victor mean by this? How was he crazed for knowledge?

❖ When Henry first hears of Victor's plan, he urges him to stop. Why doesn't he want Victor to continue with his experiment?

❖ After Victor discovers that it was the Creature who killed William, what keeps him from telling his father and Elizabeth? Do you agree with his desicion? Do you think they would have believed him? What else could he have done?

❖ In Scene 4, the Creature tells Victor, "You owe me happiness." Why does the Creature feel that Victor owes him happiness? Does the Creature's story change how you feel about him? Is the Creature truly evil?

❖ At first Victor agrees to create a companion for the Creature but later changes his mind. Why does he change his mind? What do you think would have happened if Victor had created another creature?

❖ Are there some experiments or research that scientists should not be allowed to do? Why or why not? What types of experiments should they be prohibited from doing? What areas of scientific research are controversial today?

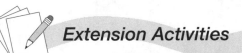

Extension Activities

A Letter to Victor

At the beginning of the play, Henry tries to convince Victor not to make the creature. Have students write a letter to Victor Frankenstein telling why he should or should not pursue his experiments. Students should include reasons to back up their point of view.

What Did the Creature Look Like?

When people think of Frankenstein's creature they generally picture the monster that appeared in the movie version. Let students use their imagination to illustrate their own version of Frankenstein's creature. Students can use the brief description in Scene 2 as their starting point. Students can create an life-size version by drawing on a large sheet of bulletin board paper.

The Modern Prometheus

The complete title of Mary Shelley's story is *Frankenstein or the Modern Prometheus*. Invite a group of students to research the myth of Prometheus. They can share their findings with the class and speculate as to how the title relates to the story.

Spooky Stories

Explain to students that Mary Shelley began writing *Frankenstein* when the poet Lord Byron challenged her and a group of friends to write ghost stories. Then extend the same challenge to your class. Students may use for inspiration any ghost stories that they know, which they can embellish in any way they see fit. Remind students that the stories should not be too violent or gory. Students can present their stories in front of the class or prepare a written version.

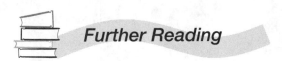

Further Reading

Students who are up for the challenge, might try reading Mary Shelley's *Frankenstein*. Other challenging gothic novels for students to try include *Rebecca* by Daphne DuMaurier, *Jane Eyre* by Charlotte Bronte and *Dracula* by Bram Stoker. All of these novels have also been adapted into movies.

The Prince and the Pauper

Adapted by Gary Drevitch from the
classic novel by Mark Twain

◆ Characters ◆

Tom Canty: 15-year-old pauper

Mr. Canty: Tom's father

Mrs. Canty: Tom's mother

Nan: Tom's sister

Neighbor

Prince Edward: 15-year-old prince

King Henry VIII: his father

Lord Hertford: a royal adviser

Lady Elizabeth: the prince's sister

Humphrey: a servant

Miles Hendon: a soldier

Hugh Hendon: his brother

Lady Edith

Blake Andrews

Officer

Guard

Narrator 1

Narrator 2

Scene 1

Narrator 1: Tom Canty was born in London in the 1530s to a poor family that did not want him.

Narrator 2: On the same day, another child was born to a rich family, who wanted him very much. That boy was Edward, Prince of Wales, first son of Henry VIII, and future King of England.

Narrator 1: Fifteen years later, Tom Canty still lived in the narrow, dirty streets of Offal Court. His father and grandmother were drunks who fought with everyone. Then they'd come home and beat Tom.

Narrator 2: They made Tom beg for them, but he refused to steal. He had learned right from wrong from his neighbor, Father Andrew, an old priest whom cruel Henry VIII had kicked out of the castle years before.

Narrator 1: Father Andrew taught Tom reading and writing. Tom's education set him apart from his friends, who jokingly treated him as their own prince.

Narrator 2: Tom's neighbors began to seek his judgement in their disputes. The wisdom of Tom's decisions always amazed the adults. He was a prince and a hero—to everyone but his own family.

Narrator 1: Tom didn't mind his life. It was all he knew. He did have one dream, though—to meet, just once, a real prince.

Scene 2

Narrator 2: And then one day, Tom's wanderings took him to Buckingham Palace. Ignoring the armed guards, Tom ran to the gate and saw the prince.

Guard (throwing Tom away from the gate): Mind your manners, beggar!

Prince: Guard! How dare you treat a poor boy like that! Open the gates, and let him in!

Guard: At once, your highness.

Prince: You look hungry. Come with me.

Narrator 2: The Prince took Tom into his room, the grandest room Tom had ever seen.

Prince: What's your name, boy?

Tom: Tom Canty, sir.

Prince: And where do you live?

Tom: In the city, sir. In Offal Court.

Prince: An odd name! Have you parents?

Tom: Yes, sir, and twin sisters, and a grandmother who is not kind to me.

Prince: She mistreats you?

Tom: Yes, sir.

Prince: Beatings?

Tom: Yes, sir.

Prince: Is your father kind to you?

Tom: No more than my grandmother.

Prince: Perhaps fathers are alike. Mine does not beat me, but he is cruel with his words. What of your mother and sisters?

Tom: They cause me no harm, sir.

Prince: I have two sisters myself—Lady Elizabeth and Lady Mary. Tell me, how do your sisters treat their servants?

Tom: We have no servants.

Prince: Then who dresses you when you wake in the morning?

Tom: Sir, we each have just one set of clothes.

Prince: How odd! But tell me—do you enjoy living in Offal Court?

Tom: Yes, sir—when I'm not hungry. The other boys and I swim in the river or wrestle.

Prince: It sounds like glorious fun! It'd be worth this entire kingdom to experience it for just a day!

Tom: Sir, it would be worth all that I have to spend just one day dressed in fine clothes like yours.

Prince: Say no more! So be it!

Narrator 1: The prince removed the Royal Seal from around his neck and put it in its hiding place. Then the boys switched clothes. Seeing each other in the prince's mirror, they realized they could be identical twins.

Prince: You have the same hair, eyes, and build as I do! No one could tell which of us was the Prince of Wales. I think that while it's fresh in my mind, I'll go punish that guard who treated you so cruelly. Don't move till I return!

Narrator 2: The prince ran downstairs in Tom's rags to find the guard.

Guard: Oh, you're back, you rotten beggar! Here, this is for the trouble you've caused me with his highness!

Narrator 1: The guard clubbed the prince and threw him out the gate.

Prince: I am the Prince of Wales! You'll hang for laying your hand on me!

Guard: Off with you, you crazy rubbish!

Narrator 2: The prince realized his mistake and ran from the castle to escape the guard. He was lost in the city until, hours later, a huge hand grabbed him by the shoulder.

Canty: Out this late, and you haven't

brought a penny home! If I don't break every bone in your body for this, then I'm not John Canty!

Prince: Oh, are you his father? Excellent! My good man, if you'll take me to the castle and fetch your boy, my father the king will make you rich beyond your wildest dreams.

Canty: You're stark raving mad, boy! But I'll beat some sense into you!

Scene 3

Narrator 2: Back at the castle, everyone thought the prince had lost his mind, or at least his memory. He didn't know his servants, his lessons, or his duties. Eventually, Henry VIII called the prince before him and his advisors.

Henry: My child, do you recognize me?

Tom (*dropping to his knees*): Sire, you are my King! I am a helpless pauper, and I pray you will believe me when I tell you I am here only by accident. I am too young to die, sire. Please, spare my life!

Henry: You'll not die, my prince!

Tom: Bless you, sire!

Henry: Hertford, the prince is ill. He's been studying too much. Let him rest and rebuild his health. But let all who live in this castle know: Be he mad or sane, Prince Edward shall still rule England after my death! Hertford, help the prince remember his life here.

Hertford: As you wish, sire.

Henry: Oh, and Hertford, the Duke of Norfolk still waits in the Tower of London for his death. Tomorrow, we'll hang him. See that the proper papers are prepared.

Hertford: If I may ask, sire, of what crime is Norfolk guilty?

Henry: Treason. I don't like the color of his hat.

Scene 4

Narrator 2: Later that day, the prince's sister, Lady Elizabeth, and his cousin, Lady Jane, came to visit Tom.

Hertford: Remember your father's order—that during your illness, you never deny that you are the Prince of Wales.

Tom: I'll remember. Please, sir—sit down.

Hertford: No, my prince. You may have forgotten: No one may sit in your presence.

Narrator 1: Tom got through his visit with Elizabeth and Jane well enough, but when their talk ended, he was surprised that no one moved to leave.

Elizabeth: Have we the permission of the prince my brother to go?

Tom: Oh! Yes, of course, anything you ask.

Narrator 2: Later that day, Henry called Hertford to him.

Henry: Let's get on with Norfolk's hanging. Bring me my Royal Seal so I can stamp these orders for the executioner.

Hertford: But my lord, you loaned the Royal Seal to Prince Edward yesterday.

Henry: Then retrieve it from the prince.

Hertford: I tried. But the prince claims not to know what the Royal Seal is.

Henry: Will the boy never get well? Postpone Norfolk's hanging until I have the Seal.

Scene 5

Narrator 1: Meanwhile, John Canty dragged the prince to his house.

Prince: I've told you: I am Edward, Prince of Wales! I do not know any of you!

Mrs. Canty: Not even your own mother?

Prince: I've never seen you before.

Canty *(sarcastically):* What a show this is! Nan, Bet, have you no manners, sitting in the presence of the Prince of Wales?

Nan: Father, Tom is worn out. He is not himself. I'm sure he'll be well tomorrow and will beg with great energy.

Prince: I will not beg. I'm not a pauper!

Narrator 2: Canty hit the prince and threw him to the floor.

Canty: I'm tired of this! Boy, you'll beg tomorrow, and you'll not come home empty-handed, if you want to walk again!

Narrator 1: Later that night, one of Canty's neighbors knocked on his door.

Neighbor: Do you know who that man was that you knocked out last night?

Canty: No, and I don't care.

Neighbor: It was old Father Andrew, and he's died of his wounds! The royal police are on their way here!

Canty: Everyone, wake up! We've got to run away! If we get separated, we'll meet at London Bridge.

Narrator 2: As everyone ran out, the prince fled into the city. Soon, he met a pack of thieves on a dark street. The thieves attacked him, but he fought back.

Prince: I am Edward, Prince of Wales! And even though I'm alone and friendless, I will stand my ground!

Narrator 1: Suddenly, a tall, muscular man appeared. He was dressed in fine, but faded, clothing and carried a sword.

Miles: I don't know if you're a prince, but you're a brave boy and you're not friendless as long as Miles Hendon is around.

Narrator 2: Miles Hendon fought off the thieves and led the Prince to safety.

Narrator 1: Meanwhile, back at the castle, Hertford had important news for Tom.

Hertford: The king is dead! *(bowing before Tom)* Long live the king!

Tom: Hertford, if I am to be king and I make a command, would it be obeyed?

Hertford: Your word is law.

Tom: Then go to the Tower of London and say that the Duke of Norfolk shall not die!

Hertford *(rushing to the Tower):* Long live Edward, king of England!

Scene 6

Narrator 2: As the prince walked with Miles past London Bridge, someone grabbed him.

Canty: Boy, you won't escape me again, not after the beating I'll give you!

Miles: What is this boy to you, brute?

Canty: He's my son. He's coming with me!

Miles: Boy, whether this scurvy fellow is your father or not, I'll see that he doesn't touch you if you'd rather stay with me.

Prince: I don't know this man, and I'd die before I'd go with him.

Miles: Then it's settled. This boy is under my protection now, so be on your way.

Narrator 1: Canty grumbled and walked away. Hendon decided to play along with the boy's story about being the prince—and, now, the king. He took him back to his rented room for dinner.

Prince: How dare you sit in my presence!

Miles *(standing):* My apologies, sire.

Prince: Your king forgives you, noble fellow. Please—tell me your story.

Miles: My mother died when I was a boy. My father is a rich and generous man. I have two brothers—my older brother Arthur, who is kind, and my younger brother Hugh, who is vicious and greedy. I haven't seen them for 10 years—since I left home to become a soldier. Seven years ago, I was captured in battle. Until days ago, I had spent all those years locked in a French prison.

Prince: So now you've returned. Does a lady wait for you at Hendon Hall?

Miles: No your majesty. The love of my life, Lady Edith, was engaged to Arthur when she was a little girl. Arthur loved someone else, but my father wouldn't let him out of the engagement. Hugh also claimed to love Lady Edith, but I think he loved only her family's wealth.

Prince: You have suffered much. I will return with you to Hendon Hall to reunite you with your family. In the meantime, you have served me well and deserve a reward. Name your desire.

Miles: It may sound odd, sire, but I request that I and my descendents forever be allowed to sit in the king's presence.

Prince: Your request is granted. Along with this: You are now Sir Miles Hendon, royal knight. Now, please sit down.

Scene 7

Narrator 2: Tom, who'd soon be crowned King, was finally getting comfortable in the castle. But the hundreds of servants still confused him—especially one.

Tom: You say you are my *whipping boy?*

Humphrey: Yes, sire. Humphrey Marlow, at your service.

Tom: As you know, Humphrey, I have a problem with my memory. Please tell me how you serve me.

Humphrey: Well, when you fail your Greek lessons, your teacher whips me—and you did fail your last test, two days ago.

Tom: You are whipped for my failings?!

Humphrey: Always, sire. Will the whippings take place today?

Tom: No. No one shall whip you today.

Humphrey: Thank you, sire! But there is one other thing—

Tom: Yes?

Humphrey: Now that you'll be king, perhaps you'll give up your studies. Then you'd never fail any more tests, and I'd be out of a job, for my back is my livelihood.

Tom: Don't worry, Humphrey. I declare you the Hereditary Grand Whipping Boy to the royal house of

England! You and your children will always have a job here!

Humphrey: Sire, you've made me so happy!

Tom: You're welcome, Humphrey. Now maybe you can help me as well. You know the prince's—I mean, my—life here in the castle as well as anyone. Let me test you on some memories that I've lost in my illness.

Narrator 1: Tom spent many hours with Humphrey. Later that day, he impressed Hertford with his returned "memory."

Hertford: I am glad to see you so well again, my Lord. Now do you remember where you put the Royal Seal?

Tom: What does this seal look like?

Hertford: Alas! You've lost your wits again! But you still have four days before you're crowned king. By then, you will be well.

Scene 8

●●●●●●●●●

Narrator: Meanwhile, Miles Hendon and the real prince arrived at Hendon Hall.

Miles: Welcome to Hendon Hall, my king! I am finally home!

Narrator 2: As they reached the gate, Miles saw his brother, Hugh.

Miles: Hugh! I have returned! Call your father to the gate, for I will not feel at home until I see his face again!

Hugh: Stranger, you seem to be out of your wits. Who do you imagine yourself to be?

Miles: Don't you recognize your brother?

Hugh: Miles?! You must be joking. I got a letter seven years ago telling me that my brother died in battle.

Miles: That's a lie! Call my father! Call Arthur! Surely they'll recognize me!

Hugh: I cannot call the dead to life.

Miles: They're both dead? I can't believe it! Lady Edith still lives, I pray.

Hugh: She lives.

Miles: Well, then, please bring her to me. She will certainly recognize me.

Narrator 1: Hugh went to find Lady Edith.

Miles: How can he say I am an impostor? I'm his own brother!

Prince: I do not doubt you, Sir Miles. But you still doubt that I am your king, do you not?

Narrator 2: At that moment, Hugh returned with Lady Edith—and a dozen armed guards.

Miles: Edith, my darling!

Hugh: Lady Edith, do you know this man?

Narrator 1: Lady Edith looked at Miles with sadness in her eyes.

Edith: I do not know him!

Hugh: Stranger, it seems you've been lying. My wife does not know you.

Miles: Your wife! Now I understand! After Father and Arthur died, you wrote the letter claiming I was dead, to steal Edith—and Hendon Hall—from me!

Narrator 2: Miles attacked Hugh, but the guards overpowered him.

Hugh: Throw him and his worthless boy into the dungeon!

Scene 9

Narrator 1: To torture Miles, Hugh sent to his cell everyone in town who once knew him. Each said that Miles was an impostor. One night, Edith visited him—with a warning.

Edith: Stranger, I know you believe you are Miles Hendon. But my husband is master of this town. If he says you are a mad impostor, then you are.

Miles: So you believe me, Edith?

Edith: I don't know you. But even if you were Miles Hendon, you would be a threat to all that Hugh has—and you would be in the same peril you are in now.

Narrator 2: One afternoon, the prison officers brought in Blake Andrews, an old man who was once Miles's servant.

Officer: Do you recognize anyone in this cell, old man?

Blake: No, all I see are street scum. Which one says he's Miles Hendon?

Officer: This big animal here.

Blake: This is not Miles Hendon!

Officer: Of course not! Why don't you give him a piece of your mind? All the others do.

Narrator 1: Blake approached Hendon and, between insults, whispered to him what he was really thinking.

Blake: You're the scum of the earth!—Sir Miles, say the word and I'll shout in the streets that you've returned—

Miles: Don't put yourself in danger.

Blake: You should be hanged!—I wish you were out of this cell. Hugh tortures Lady Edith and all the servants—

Prince: Old man, it has been so long since we've heard news from London. Has the new king been crowned yet?

Blake: You worthless beggar boy! You don't even deserve death!—King Edward will be crowned day after tomorrow. But there is a rumor going around that Edward is mad—

Prince: Mad!?

Blake: Yes, but we hear he gets better every day, and that he is wise and humane. His first acts were to spare the Duke of Norfolk and to destroy his father's cruelest laws and punishments.

Prince: How has that beggar boy fooled all the men of the castle? And learned to rule so wisely?

Narrator 2: Suddenly, the prison officers grabbed Miles and the prince.

Officer: Looks like you two are going to see daylight! Sir Hugh wants to put this impostor in the stocks so everyone can take a look at a liar.

Narrator 1: Miles was led to the town square and his arms and legs locked into the wooden frame of the stocks. The handcuffed prince looked on helplessly.

Prince: Sir Miles is a servant of the king of England! I demand you set him free!

Hugh: Officer, give the little fool a whipping to teach him to watch his tongue.

Miles: No! Let the boy go! I'll take his whipping.

Hugh: Very well.

Narrator 2: As the officers whipped Miles, the crowd grew quiet, respecting a man who would take a whipping to spare an insane boy. Hugh, realizing the people were starting to turn against him, ordered the whipping stopped.

Hugh: Stranger, you are free to leave this town. I shall return your sword and horse, but if I ever see you near Hendon Hall again, I'll have you hung!

Prince: Sir Miles, you have saved your king from public shame. Edward of England promotes you to earl.

Narrator 2: Miles was touched and began to believe that the boy actually was the king.

Miles: Your majesty, I await your command. Where shall we ride?

Prince: To London! To win back my crown!

Scene 10

Narrator 1: As Miles and the prince raced to London, Tom rode in a royal parade. Thousands of people filled the streets to look at the new king.

Tom: All these people have come to see me?!

Hertford: You are their king, and you are performing marvelously well today. You have returned to full health just in time.

Narrator 2: Suddenly, a ragged woman ran up to the royal carriage.

Mrs. Canty: Tom! I know it's you! That wasn't you at our house that night. My son!

Tom: I—I do not know you, woman.

Hertford: Officers, have this woman taken away! She offends the king.

Narrator 1: Mrs. Canty was pushed back into the crowd, and Tom stopped smiling. He was suddenly very homesick.

Hertford: My lord, don't let that crazy pauper woman disturb your great day.

Tom: She was my mother!

Narrator 2: After a day-long celebration, Tom returned to the castle. There the Archbishop of Canterbury, chief religious official of England, waited to place the crown on the head of King Edward VI.

Narrator 1: As the Archbishop raised the crown above Tom's head, another boy, dressed in rags, ran in. An older man followed.

Prince: I forbid you to set the crown of England upon that head! I am the true king!

Tom: He is! He is the king!

Miles: I must be dreaming! My little beggar boy is truly the king of England?!

Hertford: Nonsense! Your majesty, let the guards take these beggars away.

Tom: No! I order you not to touch them!

Narrator 2: Hertford suddenly noticed that the two boys were identical. He realized that he had to find a way to prove which one was the true king.

Hertford: There is one question that I know only the true Edward VI can answer: Where is the Royal Seal of England?

Narrator 1: The prince turned to one of the noblemen.

Prince: Lord St. John, I hid the Royal Seal in the helmet of the royal armor that hangs on the wall of my room.

Hertford: The beggar knows St. John's name?

Tom: You heard the king's command. Go!

Narrator 2: Lord St. John ran off and soon returned with the Royal Seal.

Hertford *(bowing to the prince):* Long live the true king!

Tom *(also bowing):* Now, my king, please take these clothes back, and give poor Tom, your servant, his shredded rags again.

Hertford: And then, guards, have this boy put to death for impersonating the king!

Prince: No! This boy is innocent of wrongdoing, and I won't punish him. I have learned much about our country's laws since I left the castle. All kings should walk as paupers for a few days to see how their laws affect the people—and so learn mercy.

Narrator 1: In all the confusion, Miles Hendon sat down next to Edward's throne.

Hertford: Stand up, you mannerless clown! You sit in the presence of the king!

Prince: Do not disturb him! It is Sir Miles' right to sit. Hertford, send the guards to capture Sir Hugh Hendon and place him in the Tower to await my punishment for theft, fraud, and cruelty. And have his wide, Lady Edith, brought here.

Narrator 2: But Sir Miles asked that Hugh Hendon not be punished. Hugh soon left England and died in Europe. After that, Miles finally married Edith.

Narrator 1: King Edward knighted Tom Canty and put him in charge of King's Hospital. With his mother and sisters, Tom watched over all the poor and sick street children of London. John Canty was never seen again.

Narrator 2: Edward VI died young after a short and merciful reign. His advisers often protested his lenient sentences of poor beggars and thieves. They said the guilty did not suffer enough, but the king always answered the same way.

Prince: What do you know of suffering? I and my people know, but you do not.

The Prince and the Pauper

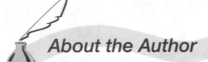

About the Author

Mark Twain is one of the most important figures in American literature, a writer known for both his humorous stories and his groundbreaking novel *The Adventures of Huckleberry Finn*. Generations of readers have enjoyed his work, including the classic stories *The Adventures of Tom Sawyer* and *The Celebrated Jumping Frog of Calaveras County*.

Mark Twain was born Samuel Langhorne Clemens in Florida, Missouri, in 1835. When he was four, he moved with his family to Hannibal, Missouri, a town on the Mississippi that inspired many of his stories. When Clemens was twelve his father died, and Clemens spent his teenage years working in a variety of jobs. He served as a printer's apprentice, piloted a steamboat on the Mississippi River, and worked as a newspaper reporter.

As a reporter, Samuel Clemens began writing funny essays and stories. He also adopted the pen name Mark Twain, which is a river expression that means "two fathoms deep." Mark Twain's career as a writer was launched with the publication of the tremendously popular *The Celebrated Jumping Frog of Calaveras County* in 1867. His reputation continued to grow with *The Innocents Abroad*, a collection of travel essays published in 1869. He completed *The Adventures of Tom Sawyer*, which was based on his childhood experiences on the Mississippi River, in 1876 and *The Prince and the Pauper* in 1881. Twain's masterpiece *The Adventures of Huckleberry Finn* was published 1884. The novel, while popular, was controversial because some critics considered the language vulgar and inappropriate—and it still causes controversy today.

Twain's other works include *A Connecticut Yankee in King Arthur's Court*, *The Tragedy of Pudd'nhead Wilson*, and *Life on the Mississippi*.

 Responding to the Play

❖ When Tom and Prince Edward first meet, the Prince is curious about Tom's life. What kinds of things does he want to know? What aspects of Tom's life does he envy?

❖ In the play, Tom Canty is puzzled by many of the traditions he encounters in the Palace. What things surprised him? Have you ever been surprised by any rules or traditions you have encountered in a new situation?

❖ In Scene 9, Prince Edward says: "How has that beggar boy fooled all the men of the castle? And learned to rule so wisely." How was Tom able to fool everyone in the castle? Why was he able to rule wisely?

❖ At the end of the play, King Edward states: "What do you know of suffering? I and my people know, but you do not." How has King Edward's experience changed him? Did Edward also act compassionately at the beginning of the play?

❖ How do you think Mark Twain viewed the monarchy in England? What does Twain portray in a positive manner and what does he seem to be making fun of?

❖ Do the characters Prince Edward and Tom share any similiar character-istics, such as intelligence or kindness? How do these traits help both characters?

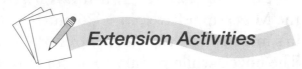

Extension Activities

The Prince and the Pauper Story Board

When directors are making movies they will sometimes create a story board that outlines the action of each scene using simple pictures. Challenge students to create a story board for "The Prince and the Pauper." Students can work in small groups to complete this project. Each group can work on one scene in the play. When all the groups have completed their story boards, post the scenes in chronological order on a bulletin board. As a finishing touch, ask each group to add a short caption that describes the action of the scene to their story board.

Learning More About the House of York

"The Prince and the Pauper" features King Henry VIII and his successor King Edward VI. Students might want to research these real-life figures to find out how accurate Twain's portrayals were. Students can begin by finding a chart that lists the successions of Kings and Queens in England. Then students can research the reign of either King Henry VIII or King Edward VI. As they research, students can also find out more about life in England during the 1500s.

Changing Places

Ask students to think about a person they would like to change places with for one day. What do they imagine that person's life is like? What would that person think of their life? Then have students write a story about trading places. Students should incorporate both their own and the other person's point-of-view in their stories. For example, if a student were to trade places with Michael Jordan, he or she should write about what it would be like to be Michael Jordan for the day and what it would be like for Michael Jordan to spend the day in his or her place. Invite students to share their stories with the class.

King or Queen for a Day

When he takes on the role of Prince, Tom has the opportunity to help people, including the Duke of Norfolk and Humphrey. Ask students what they would do if they were king or queen for the day. Students can each make a list of five things they would do if they were a ruler. Post the lists on a bulletin board for everyone to read.

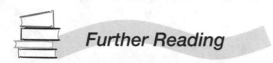

Further Reading

Other favorites by Mark Twain include the following books.

In *A Connecticut Yankee in King Arthur's Court* an inventor travels back in time to meet the knights of King Arthur's Round Table.

The Adventures of Tom Sawyer chronicles the escapades of the irrepressible Tom Sawyer.

The Lost World

Adapted from the classic novel
by Sir Arthur Conan Doyle

◆ Characters ◆

Ned Malone: a young newspaper reporter

Narrator: Ned Malone looking back

McArdle: Malone's editor at the newspaper

Professor George Challenger: a scientist
and zoologist

Professor Summerlee: a brilliant botanist
and scientist

Lord John Roxton: explorer and big-
game hunter

Mrs. Challenger: the professor's wife

Natives 1 and 2

Doda

Student

Scientists 1 and 2

Scene 1

Narrator: In my time, I've explored the four corners of the world—from the ice of the Arctic to the burning plains of Africa. But my first adventure was my greatest. It all began in the year 1910, when I was just a young reporter at the Daily Gazette in London. I was itching for The Big Story, and one night I took my request to my editor, old McArdle—a kindly old man with thick glasses and an even thicker Scottish accent.

McArdle: Mr. Malone! What brings ye here this evening, laddie?

Ned: Please, sir, I want you to send me on a special mission full of danger and adventure.

McArdle: I'm afraid that's not really your area. You're more of a city boy. But wait a wee bit—what about exposing a fraud? You could try your luck with Professor Challenger.

Ned: Challenger? The famous zoologist? What has he done?

McArdle: He came back from a solo expedition to South America last year. Refused to say exactly where he'd been, but he claimed he discovered a lost world filled with living dinosaurs. All his fellow scientists called him a fake. Here's his address. Pay him a call. Watch your step, though. He hates reporters. Most of them end the interview flying out the door, if you catch my meaning. Now, off you go!

Scene 2

Narrator: I decided to gain Challenger's confidence by posing as a scientist. When I reached the rather cluttered town house, his wife met me at the door.

Mrs. Challenger: If you've never met my husband, let me just say this: I apologize in advance. He's a perfectly terrible person.

Narrator: I didn't know what to say.

Ned: I, uh . . . Thank you for the warning, Madame.

Mrs. Challenger: If he begins to seem violent, get out of the room quickly. Don't stay and argue with him. Many have been injured by doing just that. If you can't get out, ring the bell and hold him off until I arrive . . . I just hope you're not here to talk about South America.

Narrator: I didn't have the heart to tell her that I was. Mrs. Challenger opened the door to her husband's study. There before me sat the largest, meanest-looking man I had ever seen.

Challenger: Well, what now?

Ned: Sir, I am a student of science, and I read with great interest that you claim to have found living dinosaurs in South America.

Narrator: With that, Challenger called me inside and began to yell a lecture at me. It was so filled with scientific jargon that it left me completely confused. It must have shown on my face.

Challenger: You're not a student of science! You're a vile, crawling journalist. A creeping vermin. Did you really think you could match wits with me? With your walnut of a brain?

Narrator: And with that, he socked me, a straight right to the jaw, knocking me out cold. When I awoke, I was sitting outside Challenger's house with a note pinned to my jacket. It read: "If you are truly interested in my ideas about South America, come to my lecture tonight at Ainsley Lecture Hall."

Scene 3

Narrator: I arrived at the lecture hall. White-bearded professors and noisy students packed the room. When Professor Challenger came onstage, the crowd whooped and hissed loudly at him.

Challenger *(addressing the crowd):* My idiotic colleagues say that prehistoric animals no longer exist. I tell you that dinosaurs are alive today—monsters that could devour our largest and fiercest mammals.

Student: Liar! Where's your proof?

Challenger *(to the crowd):* Now listen to me, you howling mob of hooligans who call yourselves scientists: Since you don't believe my claims, I will put you to the test. Who among you will come on an expedition to South America to investigate my statements?

Narrator: A scientist in the crowd leaped to his feet.

Summerlee: Professor Challenger, tell us exactly where these prehistoric animals are to be found.

Challenger: I will give that information only on the way to South America. I don't suppose you would volunteer?

Summerlee: Oh, yes, I will—to prove what a fraud you are.

Challenger: Fine. Anyone else?

Narrator: Here was my chance for adventure! I stood up.

Ned: I'll go, sir! My name is Ned Malone. We met this afternoon.

Challenger: You?! Well done, my boy. I may just get to like you yet.

Narrator: Another man stood.

Roxton: Me, sir, I'm Lord John

Roxton. I hunt big game and I've been up and down the Amazon.

Challenger: So be it. Gentlemen, you have one week to get ready for the adventure of your lives!

Scene 4

Narrator: In those days, of course, we couldn't hop on a plane to Rio. Instead, we took an ocean liner to Brazil. There we traveled up the Amazon by steamer, canoe, and finally, on foot through the jungle. Lord Roxton was terrific—he knew all the ins and outs, a jolly chap. But the old rivals, Challenger and Summerlee, argued the entire journey like two children. At last, we arrived at our destination: a strange bare meadow with a huge plateau looming in front of us. It looked rather like a large tree stump.

Challenger: Up there is our lost world, men. We'll camp here for the night. Summerlee, you start a fire, and Ned can cook the wild pig Lord Roxton shot for our supper.

Summerlee: I ask you, sir: What gives you the authority to issue there orders?

Challenger: I issue orders because I am leader of this expedition!

Narrator: Roxton gave me a crafty smile. We both knew that the two old

scientists could drag this argument out all night.

Roxton: Here we go again, Ned.

Ned: Guess I'll make the fire.

Narrator: As Roxton scurried all around making camp for the night, Summerlee and Challenger sat on a large rock and bickered.

Summerlee: Mr. Challenger, you are not the leader. You are a man whose reputation is on trial. We, sir, are your judges.

Challenger: You, sir, are barely fit to make my campfire. If your tiny brain was even the size of my fist . . .

Narrator: Suddenly Roxton pointed to something on a nearby cliff.

Roxton: What the devil is that? There, on that rocky ridge!

Challenger: It's-It's a pterodactyl!

Summerlee: Ha! Is this what you brought us here to see? That's a stork.

Ned: Something's out there! I can hear it! Look out! It's coming straight for us!

Narrator: We ran for cover, but I saw the creature's leathery wings, a snake-like neck, greedy red eyes, and a great snapping beak with rows of little, gleaming teeth.

Challenger: It's gone.

Roxton: And so is our supper. The beastie flew off with our pig!

Summerlee *(shaken):* Professor Challenger, I owe you an apology.

Challenger: Accepted, sir. Now, to bed, for tomorrow, we enter The Lost World!

Scene 5

Narrator: Climbing the sheer, glassy walls of the plateau proved impossible, but at last we found our way up a slender rock tower. On the tower there was a tall, strong tree that we chopped down to make a bridge over to the plateau. It was a historic moment—the first step into a new world.

Challenger: I claim the honor to be the first to cross.

Roxton: Sorry, Professor. When it is a matter of science, I follow your lead. But it's up to you to follow me now. We are invading a new country, which may be chock-full of enemies. Could be cannibals waiting for lunch over there. I don't want to follow you into a cooking pot.

Narrator: Roxton ran across the log with two rifles strapped to his back and another in hand. The professors and I, however, scooted across the log-bridge on our bottoms, trying not to look down.

Roxton: Quiet, everyone! So long as neither man nor beast sees or hears us, we're safe. Let's get a good look at all our neighbors before we decide to get on visiting terms.

Narrator: We walked silently through a hundred yards of forest before we made our discovery.

Roxton: Look at these tracks—three-toed, and enormous. By George, this must be the father of all birds! I'll bet it passed here not more than 10 minutes ago . . .

Narrator: Roxton's words died into a whisper. Before us were five extraordinary dinosaurs—two adults and three young, with shiny skin like a lizard's.

Challenger: Put it down in your notes, Ned. On August the 28th we saw five iguanodons.

Ned: This is going to be the biggest story ever written!

Summerlee: What will they say back in England at the lecture hall!

Challenger: That you are a liar and a scientific phony, exactly as you said of me.

Summerlee: But when I show them photographs . . .

Challenger: They'll call them fakes.

Summerlee: Then we must bring back

a specimen!

Challenger: If only we could get one.

Roxton *(determined):* I'll get you a specimen, or my name's not John Roxton. As for me, I'd dearly love to take one of those heads with me. I know a few hunters that would turn green with envy if they saw one of those mounted on my wall!

Scene 6

Narrator: That night I slipped out of camp to have an adventure all my own. I followed a brook to a great lake. Dinosaurs swam about, diving for food. Then, in the cliffs across the lake, I saw caves with fires burning. There were humans in The Lost World! I raced back to camp—only to find it in ruins. A pool of blood stained the grass. My friends were nowhere in sight. I must have fainted. The next thing I knew, Roxton knelt beside me, cut and bruised, but very much alive.

Roxton: Quick, young fella! Every moment counts. Get those rifles and all the cartridges you can carry. Get a move on. They're on our trail for sure!

Ned: I'm coming fast as I can, but who is following us?

Roxton: Missing Links, Challenger

calls them. I wish they'd stayed missing. What brutes! Early this morning they rained down on us from the trees, screaming and swinging stone clubs. I shot one in the belly and kicked and scratched until I got away.

Ned: But the professors!

Roxton: Prisoners. I came back here to get our guns and try a rescue. I'm glad you're with me, Ned. We're nearly there—see them all gathered there, at the edge of the cliff? Make peace with your soul, for this will be a fight to the death.

Narrator: I saw a hundred huge, shaggy, red-haired creatures. They had humanlike faces bristling with coarse whickers. Their eyes, under heavy brows, were ferocious. They had curved, sharp canine teeth. The professors were their prisoners, all right—but they were not alone. I saw five other humans, short of limb, with dark bronze skins. I knew they must be the humans whose fires I had seen in the caves by the lake. These natives hated and feared their captors.

Roxton: Look, Ned. They've got one of the little humans on the edge of the cliff! Great heavens, they've tossed the poor wretch over!

Ned: They've got Summerlee—he's going to be next!

Roxton: Shoot into the thick of them!

Shoot, lad, shoot!

Narrator: The crack of our guns confused and frightened the creatures. They ran for the woods and left us alone with the four surviving natives, who trembled with fear. One darted forward and threw his arms around Roxton's legs.

Roxton: By George! Get up, fella, and take your face off my boots.

Summerlee: He's grateful. You and young Ned here pulled us all out of the jaws of death.

Challenger: European science owes you both a deep debt of gratitude. My death—and Summerlee's, of course—would have been a terrible blow to modern zoological history. Now, as for these poor men, we must take them home—if only we knew where their home is.

Ned: I was there last night. They live on the other side of a great lake not far from here.

Roxton: We must move then, and move quickly, before those creatures decide to follow us.

Scene 7

Narrator: We set off at once. The natives were small men, wiry and well-built. We couldn't understand their language. One of them pointed at himself, and then his three friends.

Native 1: Accala. Accala, Accala, Accala.

Ned: OK. You are Accala.

Native 2: Grrrrr! Doda! Doda! Grrr!

Roxton: Well, that's clear enough. Doda—that's the creatures, the enemy.

Ned: I'm NED. We're BRITISH.

Roxton: Where do you think these Accala came from, Professor?

Challenger: They certainly are not from the same family as their enemies. I would say they came here centuries, maybe millennia ago, from the Brazilian valley.

Ned: That's the lake up ahead.

Summerlee: And look there! A whole flotilla of canoes!

Roxton: More of these Accalas—and every one of them's got a spear or a bow. Watch yourselves, mates. We could be in for it. Hey there, don't touch that gun!

Native: Doda! Doda!

Ned: I don't think they're after us. They're going to fight the Doda.

Challenger: Excellent deduction, my dear boy. Your intelligence seems to be improving in my company. Now then—say, there, don't be pulling on my sleeve.

Native 2: Doda! Doda!

Ned: I think they want us to fight with them.

Roxton: I'm inclined to help. What do you say, Ned?

Ned: I'm in.

Challenger: I will certainly cooperate. In the name of science, of course.

Summerlee: Science? This is a tribal war. It's not science! Still, if you all are going, I don't see how I can remain behind.

Roxton: Then it's settled. Doda. Doda!

Natives: Doda! Doda!

Scene 8

Narrator: We set upon our enemy at dawn the next day. We didn't have to travel far. Soon we were engaged in a fierce battle.

Doda: Aaaaaaiiiieeeee!

Roxton: We're in it now, men! For the love of God and your country, fight on!

Native 1: Accala! ACCALA!

Ned: Enemy straight ahead, watch it, Roxton!

Roxton: Take that, you murdering fiend!

Summerlee: Help!

Challenger: Easy, Summerlee! I'm right behind you!

Ned: Ha! Got one! If I live through this, I'm going to be a war reporter!

Roxton: That's the spirit, lad—watch out!

Narrator: Screaming and howling, the Doda rushed away in all directions. The Accala yelled in delight, following swiftly after them. I started to follow them, but Roxton stopped me.

Roxton: It's over, lad. I think we can leave the tidying up to the Accala. The less we see of that mess, the better we'll sleep.

Challenger: Gentlemen, we have been privileged to be present at the kind of battle which determines the fate of the world. Survival of the fittest! Now, upon this plateau, the future will forever be that of man.

Summerlee: Very nice, sir. But from now on, we must devote all our energy to getting out of this country and back to civilization. Is that clear?

Challenger: You, sir, seem to care less about science and more about your slippers and your tea.

Summerlee: Nonsense.

Scene 9

Narrator: We sailed back to London and soon took the stage at the same lecture hall where our expedition had begun. Summerlee reported our findings to the scientists: the dinosaurs we observed, and the Doda and Accala. Many cheered, but there were still some people who didn't believe us.

Scientist 1: First Challenger came here with his strange stories. Now you four return with even stranger ones. Where's your evidence?

Summerlee: We have photos. We have reports from a member of the press.

Scientist 2: Photos can be faked. And newspaper stories don't prove anything.

Challenger: Well, then. If it's proof you want—gentlemen, here it is!

Narrator: Roxton and I carried onstage a large crate. A hush fell over the audience.

Challenger (*talking into the crate*): Come, then, pretty, pretty!

Narrator: A pterodactyl perched on the side of the crate. The audience went berserk—hundreds of people gasped and screamed, and two ladies in the front row fell senseless from their chairs.

Roxton: Stop screaming! You're frightening the poor beastie!

Ned: Challenger, quick—it's about to fly. Grab its legs!

Narrator: Too late. The pterodactyl circled the hall faster and faster, beating its wings against walls and chandeliers in a blind frenzy.

Challenger: The window! For heaven's sake shut that window!

Narrator: The creature squeezed its hideous bulk through the window and was gone. The audience suddenly rose up in cheers. We four were carried into the street for a real heroes' reception. As for our London pterodactyl, it perched on the Queen's Hall for a few hours, and then headed south and west, over the Atlantic-perhaps trying to find its home again, far away in The Lost World.

The Lost World

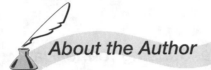

About the Author

Mystery fans know Sir Arthur Conan Doyle from his famous detective Sherlock Holmes. But as "The Lost World" demonstrates, Doyle was a versatile author who also wrote adventure stories, plays, and nonfiction.

Doyle was born in Edinburgh, Scotland, in 1859. After graduating from Edinburgh University's School of Medicine, he practiced medicine in England.

In 1887, Doyle published his first story, "A Study in Scarlett," which featured the brillant detective Sherlock Holmes. Doyle based the Sherlock Holmes character on a doctor who was known for his ability to quickly diagnose patients. After writing more than 20 Sherlock Holmes stories, Doyle killed off his famous dectective in the story "The Final Problem." But Sherlock Holmes fans still wanted more and eventually Doyle brought the dectective back to solve more crimes.

In 1902, Doyle wrote a highly regarded book about Britain's Boer War, *The War in South Africa: Its Causes and Conduct,* which defended Britain's actions during the Boer War. Doyle was later knighted for this effort, as well as for his service as a doctor during the war.

The Lost World is one three science-fiction novels that Doyle wrote featuring the scientist Professor Challenger. The other books were *The Poison Belt* and *The Land of Mist*. Doyle also wrote historical fiction, including the novels *Micha Clarke* and *The White Company*. Later in life, Doyle became interested in spiritualism and wrote many books about the subject.

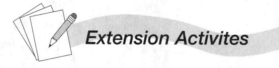

Responding to the Play

❖ Why didn't Challenger like Ned at first? Did Challenger change his mind about Ned during the course of the play?

❖ Which of the characters was most helpful in the Lost World? Why? Who was the least helpful?

❖ At the end of the play, what kind of proof did the men have to provide to convince other scientists and the public that the dinosaurs were real?

❖ Could a Lost World really exisit? Why or why not? If it could, in what part of the world could it exist? Are there any parts of the world that are so remote that they are nearly impossible to get to? Are there any places that are uninhabited by man? Could a Lost World exist in one of those spots?

Extension Activites

Extra! Extra! Dinosaurs Discovered!

Remind students that in this story the narrator was a newspaper reporter. Have students act as reporters and write a newspaper article about the events in the play. Explain to students that their articles should start with a snappy lead that will grab a reader's attention and include four or five paragraphs that clearly explain all the key facts. Students should be sure to add a headline to their final story.

Trekking to the Amazon

In the play the narrator notes that to get to the Lost World in the Amazon, they had to take an ocean liner, canoe, and, finally, go on foot. Challenge students to find the Amazon on a world map, figure out how they could get there today and estimate how long it would take them. Then, have them figure out how they could get there without taking a plane and how long that would take them.

Character Monologues

To give students a new view on the play, have them prepare short character monologues. Each student should pick one character and write a short speech in the character's voice. The speech should include the character's major achievements and also convey the character's personality. Students can use the descriptive information presented in the play as a starting point and then invent additional information about the characters to fill out their portraits.

Design a Poster Advertising the Play

Students can demonstrate their understanding of the play by designing a poster advertising it. The posters should feature the play's title, a tagline that states what the story is about, and an illustration that depicts an exciting part of the story. Students can also choose contemporary actors to portray different characters.

Further Reading

Professor Challenger is also featured in two more of Doyle's books, *The Poison Belt* and *The Land of Mist*.

Mystery fans are sure to enjoy Doyle's classic Sherlock Holmes tales, including *The Hound of Baskervilles*, *The Adventures of Sherlock Holmes*, and *The Memoirs of Sherlock Holmes*.

Notes